Elements of Litera

Second Course

Holt Adapted Reader

from *Elements of Literature*
- **Adapted Literary Selections**
- **Poetry and Drama Selections**
- **Adapted Informational Texts**

HOLT, RINEHART AND WINSTON

A Harcourt Education Company

Orlando • **Austin** • New York • San Diego • Toronto • London

CREDITS

Executive Editor: Katie Vignery

Senior Editor: Amy Strong

Editor: Nicole Svobodny

Copyediting: Michael Neibergall, *Copyediting Manager;* Kristen Azzara, Mary Malone, *Copyediting Supervisors;* Christine Altgelt, Elizabeth Dickson, Leora Harris, Anne Heausler, Kathleen Scheiner, *Senior Copyeditors;* Emily Force, Julia Thomas Hu, Nancy Shore, *Copyeditors*

Project Administration: Marie Price, *Managing Editor;* Elizabeth LaManna, *Associate Managing Editor;* Janet Jenkins, *Senior Editorial Coordinator;* Christine Degollado, Betty Gabriel, Mark Koenig, Erik Netcher, *Editorial Coordinators*

Permissions: Ann Farrar, *Senior Permissions Editor*

Design: Richard Metzger, Betty Mintz

Production: Beth Prevelige, *Senior Production Manager;* Carol Trammel, *Production Manager;* Leanna Ford, Belinda Barbosa Lopez, Michael Roche, *Senior Production Coordinators;* Dolores Keller, Carol Marunas, *Production Coordinators;* Myles Gorospe, *Production Assistant*

Publishing Services: Laura Likon, *Technical Services Director;* Juan Baquera, *Technical Services Manager;* Margaret Sanchez, *Senior Technical Services Analyst*

Manufacturing: Shirley Cantrell, *Manufacturing Supervisor;* Mark McDonald, *Inventory Analyst;* Amy Borseth, *Manufacturing Coordinator*

Printed in the United States of America

ISBN 0-03-035712-8

1 2 3 4 5 6 7 179 05 04 03

Contents

Reading Literature and Informational Texts

Skills Table of Contents

Reading Skills

Literary Skills

Vocabulary Skills

PHOTO CREDITS

Abbreviations used: (tl) top left, (tc) top center, (tr) top right, (l) left, (lc) left center, (c) center, (rc) right center, (r) right, (bl) bottom left, (bc) bottom center, (br) bottom right, (bkgd) background.

Page 8 (border), 9–10, Digital Image copyright © 2005 PhotoDisc; 22 (bkgd), 23–26, Digital Image copyright © 2005 PhotoDisc; 28 (border), © Arthur Rothstein/CORBIS; 29 (bl), © Bettmann/CORBIS; 29 (br), Digital Image copyright © 2005 Artville; 29 (bkgd), 30–34, © Arthur Rothstein/CORBIS; 43–44, © Layne Kennedy/CORBIS; 48 (c), © Chip Simons Photography; 48 (bc), © CORBIS; 48 (br), © Reuters NewMedia Inc./CORBIS; 48 (bl), © Roger Ressmeyer/CORBIS; 49 (tr), National Geographic Society; Artwork © David B. Mattingly; 49 (bl), National Geographic Society; 50 (border), 51, © Mark Richards/PhotoEdit; 52–55, Digital Image copyright © 2005 PhotoDisc; 59 (bl), © Bettmann/CORBIS; 59 (br), Courtesy United Farm Workers; 59 (cr & tr), © Bettmann/CORBIS; 59 (tl), Arthur Schatz/Time Life Picture Collection/Getty Images; 60, © Bettmann/CORBIS; 63 (c), © Bob LeRoy/Index Stock Imagery, Inc. 63 (bkgd), 64, Digital Image copyright © 2005 PhotoDisc; 67 (bkgd), © AFF/AFS Amsterdam/The Netherlands/Archive Photos/Getty Images; 67 (c), 68–88 (t), © AFF/AFS Amsterdam/The Netherlands/Hulton Archive/Getty Images; 90 (border), 91 (bkgd), Grant Heilman Photography, Inc.; 91 (tl, tr, & cl), © Seattle Post-Intelligencer Collection; Museum of History and Industry/CORBIS; 92–96, Grant Heilman Photography, Inc.; 99 (tc), The Granger Collection, New York.; 99 (bkgd), 98 (border), 100, H. Mark Weidman; 102 (border), 103 (bkgd), © Don Uhbrock/Time Life Picture Collection/Getty Images; 103, 104, © UPI/Bettmann/CORBIS; 107 (cl), © CORBIS; 107 (bc & bkgd), Matt Heron/Black Star; 108–109, © CORBIS; 113 (bkgd), © Telegraph Colour Library/Getty Images; 120–125, HRW Photo; 132–141, Digital Image copyright © 2005 PhotoDisc; 144 (border), HRW Illustration; 145 (t), © Tom Walker/Getty Images; 145 (bkgd), 146–153, HRW Illustration; 157–160, The Granger Collection, New York.; 163–164, Robert W. Kelley/Time Life Picture Collection/Getty Images; 167 (t), © Jim Erichson/CORBIS; 167 (c), Tony Hutchings/Getty Images; 168–172 & 175–176, Tony Hutchings/Getty Images; 178 (border), Digital Image copyright © 2005 PhotoDisc; 179 (bkgd), © UPI/Bettmann/CORBIS; 179 (tr & l), Digital Image copyright © 2005 PhotoDisc; 180–184, Digital Image copyright © 2005 PhotoDisc; 187 (tl), Robert Bossi/Getty Images; 187 (tr), Time Life Picture Collection/Getty Images; 187 (bl), Cameron Davidson/Getty Images; 187 (br), © Michael S. Yamashita/ CORBIS; 187 (bkgd), Digital Image copyright © 2005 PhotoDisc; 188 (l), Cameron Davidson/Getty Images; 188 (r), Time Life Picture Collection/Getty Images; 189–190, Cameron Davidson/Getty Images; 192–200, Digital Image copyright © 2005 PhotoDisc.

To the Student

A Book for You

Imagine this. A book full of great stories and interesting informational articles. Make it a book that actually tells you to write in it. Fill it with graphic organizers. Make it a size that's easy to carry around. That's *Holt Adapted Reader*—a book created especially for you.

In *Holt Adapted Reader,* you will find two kinds of selections—original selections and adaptations.

Adaptations are based on stories or articles that appear in *Elements of Literature,* Second Course. Adaptations make the selections more accessible to all readers. You can easily identify any selection that is an adaptation. Just look for the words "based on" in the Table of Contents or on selection opening pages.

Original selections are exactly what appear in *Elements of Literature,* Second Course. The poems and play in this book are examples of original selections. With the poetry and drama selections, you may find two kinds of help — **YOU NEED TO KNOW** and **IN OTHER WORDS**. You Need to Know gives you background information about the work. It also explains some of the work's main ideas. In Other Words paraphrases the text that comes before it. That is, it restates the text in different words.

Holt Adapted Reader is designed to accompany *Elements of Literature.* Like *Elements of Literature,* it's designed to help you interact with the literature and informational materials you read.

Learning to Read Literary and Informational Texts

When you read informational materials, you usually read to get the facts. You read mainly to get information that is stated directly on the page. When you read literature, you need to go beyond the words on the page. You need to read between the lines of a poem or story to discover the writer's meaning. No matter what kind of reading you do, *Holt Adapted Reader* will help you practice the skills and strategies you need to become an active and successful reader.

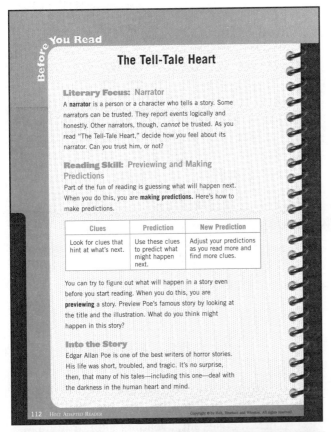

Before You Read

The Before You Read page previews the skill or skills you will practice as you read the selection.

- In the **Literary Focus**, you will learn about one literary element—like character or rhyme. This literary element is one you will see in the selection.
- The **Reading Skill** presents a key skill you will need to read the selection.

The Before You Read page also introduces you to the reading selection.

- **Into the Story** (or **Poem,** or **Article**) gives you background information. This information will help you understand the selection or its author. It may also help you understand the time period in which the selection was written.

Interactive Selections from
Elements of Literature

The selections in *Holt Adapted Reader* also appear in *Elements of Literature,* Second Course. Most are adaptations of these selections. The selections are reprinted in a single column. They are also printed in larger type to give you the room you need to mark up the text.

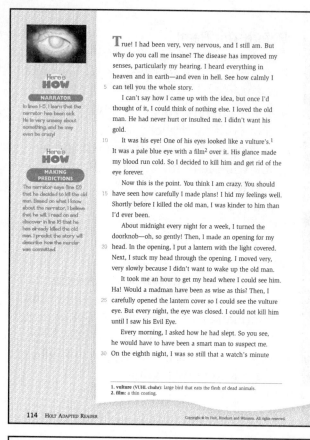

Here's HOW

NARRATOR

In lines 1–5, I learn that the narrator has been sick. He is very uneasy about something, and he may even be crazy!

Here's HOW

MAKING PREDICTIONS

The narrator says (line 12) that he decided to kill the old man. Based on what I know about the narrator, I believe that he will. I read on and discover in line 16 that he has already killed the old man. I predict the story will describe how the murder was committed.

True! I had been very, very nervous, and I still am. But why do you call me insane? The disease has improved my senses, particularly my hearing. I heard everything in heaven and in earth—and even in hell. See how calmly I
5 can tell you the whole story.

I can't say how I came up with the idea, but once I'd thought of it, I could think of nothing else. I loved the old man. He had never hurt or insulted me. I didn't want his gold.

10 It was his eye! One of his eyes looked like a vulture's.[1] It was a pale blue eye with a film[2] over it. His glance made my blood run cold. So I decided to kill him and get rid of the eye forever.

Now this is the point. You think I am crazy. You should
15 have seen how carefully I made plans! I hid my feelings well. Shortly before I killed the old man, I was kinder to him than I'd ever been.

About midnight every night for a week, I turned the doorknob—oh, so gently! Then, I made an opening for my
20 head. In the opening, I put a lantern with the light covered. Next, I stuck my head through the opening. I moved very, very slowly because I didn't want to wake up the old man.

It took me an hour to get my head where I could see him. Ha! Would a madman have been as wise as this? Then, I
25 carefully opened the lantern cover so I could see the vulture eye. But every night, the eye was closed. I could not kill him until I saw his Evil Eye.

Every morning, I asked how he had slept. So you see, he would have to have been a smart man to suspect me.
30 On the eighth night, I was so still that a watch's minute

1. **vulture** (VUHL chuhr): large bird that eats the flesh of dead animals.
2. **film:** a thin coating.

---

hand moves faster than my hand. Before this moment, I had never felt how powerful and wise I was. The old man moved on the bed suddenly, as if he had been startled.[3]

Now, you may think that I drew back, but I knew that he
35 could not see the door opening in the dark. Finally, I had my head in. My thumb slipped on the lantern's cover. The old man cried out, "Who's there?"

I kept still for a whole hour. During that time the old man sat up in bed, listening. Then, I heard a groan of terror. At
40 midnight on many nights, I have made that sound. I pitied the old man, but my heart chuckled.

I knew that he had been lying awake since the first noise. He had been growing more and more afraid. But there was no escape. The presence of Death made him *feel* my head in
45 the room.

I waited for a long time, very patiently. I aimed the light only on the old man's vulture eye. It was wide open.

Now, I have told you that I am not mad. Rather, my senses are too sharp. So I began to hear a low, dull, quick
50 sound, like a watch wrapped in cotton. I knew *that* sound too well. It was the beating of the old man's heart. It made me even angrier, like a drumbeat makes a soldier braver.

I held the light on the eye, but the sound of the heart grew quicker and louder. He *must* have been terrified![4] The
55 noise terrified me, too. I thought the heart would burst. And now I became afraid that a neighbor might hear the sound.

With a loud yell, I leaped into the bedroom. The old man shrieked only once. In an instant, I dragged him to the floor and pulled the heavy bed over him. Then, I smiled because
60 the deed[5] was done.

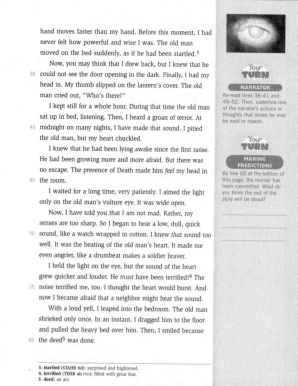

Your TURN

NARRATOR

Re-read lines 38–41 and 48–52. Then, underline one of the narrator's actions or thoughts that shows he may be mad or insane.

Your TURN

MAKING PREDICTIONS

By line 60 at the bottom of this page, the murder has been committed. What do you think the rest of the story will be about?

_____

_____

_____

3. **startled** (STAHR tld): surprised and frightened.
4. **terrified** (TEHR uh fyd): filled with great fear.
5. **deed:** an act.

Side Notes

The **Here's HOW** feature models, or shows you, how to apply a particular skill to what you are reading. This feature lets you see how another reader might think about the text. You can figure out the focus of a Here's HOW by looking in the green oval under the heading. Each Here's HOW focuses on a reading skill, a literary skill, or a vocabulary skill.

The **Your TURN** feature gives you a chance to practice a skill on your own. Each Your TURN focuses on a reading skill, a literary skill, or a vocabulary skill. You might be asked to underline or circle words in the text. You might also be asked to write your response on lines that are provided for you.

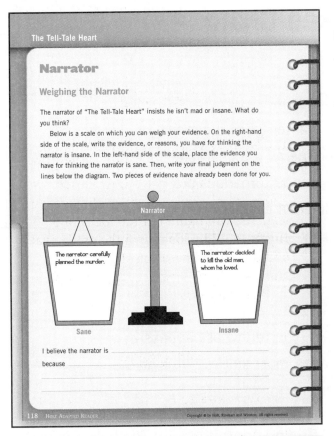

Graphic Organizers

After each selection, **graphic organizers** give you a visual way to understand the reading or literary focus of the selection. You might be asked to evaluate the narrator, chart the main events of the plot, or complete a cause-and-effect chain.

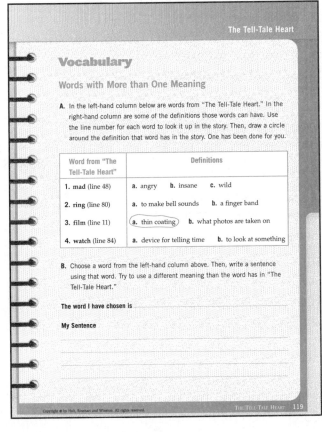

Vocabulary

Vocabulary worksheets at the end of some selections check your knowledge of vocabulary words. They also check your understanding of the selection.

Broken Chain

Literary Focus: Conflict

In every short story, the main character faces a **conflict,** or problem. **External conflicts** are problems the character faces on the outside: Battles with dragons or tornadoes are examples of external conflicts. **Internal conflicts** occur inside a character. Shyness, fear, jealousy—these kinds of feelings cause internal conflicts.

Reading Skill: Summarizing a Plot

When you **summarize** a story's plot, you tell what happens in your own words. You can summarize most stories by using a *somebody / wants / but / so* chart.

Somebody: main character	Little Red Riding Hood
Wants: what the character wants	wants to take a basket of food to her Grandmother
But: problems (or **conflicts**) the character has getting what she wants	but the Big Bad Wolf eats Grandmother and tries to eat Little Red Riding Hood
So: how it all works out in the end	so Little Red Riding Hood screams and is rescued by a nearby woodman and his ax.

Into the Story

The author of this story, Gary Soto, brings to life the Mexican American neighborhood in which he grew up. Parts of this story are based on Soto's life. He would have liked to have had a girlfriend to ride bikes with. Instead, he says, he had to give bike rides to his younger brother.

Broken Chain

Chain

Based on the Story by
Gary Soto

1   **A**lfonso's teeth were crooked, like a pile of wrecked cars. He sat on the porch trying to push his teeth to where he thought they belonged. When he stopped pushing his teeth, he wiped down his bike with an old gym sock.

5   Alfonso's older brother, Ernie, rode up on his bicycle, parked it, and sat with his head down, sullen[1] as a toad.

  Alfonso knew better than to say anything. He sat and compared the two bikes. His gleamed like a handful of dimes, while Ernie's looked dirty.

10   Finally Ernie groaned and said, "Ah, man."

  Alfonso waited a few minutes before asking, "What's the matter?"

  "Those girls didn't show up. And you better not laugh."

  "What girls?"

15   Then Alfonso remembered his brother bragging about how he and Frostie met two girls last week on Halloween night.

  "They said we were supposed to wait at the corner," said Ernie. "But they didn't show up. Me and Frostie waited

20 and waited. . . . They were playing games[2] with us."

  "Were they cute?" Alfonso asked.

  "I guess so," said Ernie.

  Alfonso sat with his brother in silence. Girls could sure act weird.

25   After a while, Alfonso pedaled his bike up the street. At his old elementary school, he found a kid hanging upside down on the barbed-wire fence. A girl looked up at the kid.

---

1. sullen (SUHL uhn): unpleasantly silent.
2. playing games: tricking.

"Broken Chain" adapted from *Baseball in April and Other Stories* by Gary Soto. Copyright © 1990 by Gary Soto. Retold by Holt, Rinehart and Winston. Reproduced by permission of **Harcourt, Inc.**

Alfonso stopped and helped the kid untangle his pants from the barbed wire. The kid was grateful. His sister, who was

30 Alfonso's age, was also grateful.

"Thanks," she said. "What's your name?"

"Alfonso." She was kind of cute, with ponytails and straight teeth. "You go to my school, huh?"

"Yeah. I've seen you around."

35 Alfonso walked along as the girl and her brother started for home. They didn't talk much. Every few steps, the girl, whose name was Sandra, would look at him out of the corner of her eye. Alfonso would look away.

Alfonso and Sandra stopped at the corner of her street.

40 Her brother ran on home.

"I live over there," she said, pointing.

Alfonso looked down at his feet for a long time, trying to get up enough nerve[3] to ask her to go bike riding. At last he looked up at her and asked shyly, "You want to go bike

45 riding?"

"Maybe." She played with a ponytail. "But my bike has a flat."

"I can get my brother's bike. How about after school on Monday?"

50 "I have to take care of my brother until my mom comes home from work. How about four-thirty?"

"OK," he said. "Four-thirty." Alfonso took off on his bike, jumped the curb, and, cool as he could be, raced away with his hands stuffed in his pockets. But when he looked back

55 over his shoulder, Sandra wasn't even looking.

That night he took a bath, brushed his hair, and did more than his usual set of exercises. In bed, after pushing on his teeth, he asked Ernie to let him borrow his bike.

---

3. get up enough nerve: be brave enough.

VOCABULARY

The word *untangle* (line 28) looks strange to me. If I break it up, though, I see that it has two parts: *un* and *tangle*. I know that the prefix *un-* means "reverse the action." The word *untangle* must mean "to get something out of a tangle." I think the tangle is where the kid's pants got caught on the wire.

SUMMARIZING

In lines 42–45, we find out one thing that Alfonso *wants* in this story. What is it?

_____

_____

_____

But—read on (lines 46–49): What could keep him from getting what he wants? Do you think this problem will be easy to overcome? Explain.

_____

_____

_____

_____

"Who's going to use it?"

60 Alfonso paused, then decided to tell the truth. "I met this girl."

Ernie rolled over on his stomach and stared at his brother. "*You* got a girlfriend?"

"She ain't my girlfriend, just a girl."

65 "What does she look like?"

"She's got ponytails and a little brother."

"Ponytails! Those girls who messed with Frostie and me had ponytails." Ernie sat up in bed. "I bet you that's her. I'm going to get even with her!"

70 "You better not touch her," Alfonso snarled. "I'll run you over with my bike."

For the next hour, they fought over whether she was the girl who had stood Ernie up. Alfonso said that she was too nice to pull a trick[4] like that. Ernie said the girl who stood

75 him up was in the same grade and had ponytails. Secretly, Ernie was jealous.[5] He did not want his younger brother to have a girlfriend.

Sunday morning at breakfast, Ernie and Alfonso fought over the last tortilla. At church they made faces at one

80 another. Ernie punched Alfonso in the arm, and Alfonso, his eyes wide with anger, punched back.

Monday at school, Alfonso worried himself sick about borrowing a bike for Sandra. Should he ask his best friend, Raul, for his bike? But Alfonso knew Raul, a paperboy with

85 dollar signs in his eyes, would charge[6] him, and he had less than sixty cents.

---

4. **pull a trick:** to try to fool; play a joke on.
5. **jealous** (JEHL uhs): wanting what someone else has.
6. **charge:** ask to be paid money for.

All day, Alfonso avoided Sandra. After school, he
hurried home and did his chores. He did a hundred sit-ups,
pushed on his teeth until they hurt, showered, and combed
90 his hair. He then stepped out to the patio to clean his bike.
Suddenly, he decided to remove the chain and wipe off the
dirty oil. But the chain broke while he was unhooking it. It
lay in his hand like a dead snake.

Alfonso couldn't believe his luck. He did not have an
95 extra bike for Sandra. Now, he had no bike for himself. He
threw the chain down on the cement, and it broke in another
place. It popped up and hit him, stabbing at his hand like a
snake's fang.[7]

"Ow!" he cried. He dabbed some iodine[8] on his cut. It
100 only hurt more. What was he to do? Again Alfonso begged
his brother for his bike, and again his brother refused.

How could he face Sandra with no bike? At four, he
decided to get it over with. He trudged slowly toward
Sandra's house, as if he were waist-deep in water. Why did
105 he have to take the chain off? he scolded himself. Now he
had to tell Sandra, "I broke my bike, and my mean brother
won't lend me his." She might laugh. She might even call
him *menso*—stupid.

At the corner where they were supposed to meet, he
110 hid behind a hedge.[9] No one was outside her house. Just
as he was thinking about going home, he heard footsteps.
He peeked through the hedge. She was standing on tiptoe
to see if he was coming around the corner.

What have I done? Alfonso thought. He bit his lip,
115 called himself *menso,* and pounded his palm against his
forehead. Someone slapped the back of his head. He
turned around and there was Ernie.

---

7. **fang:** tooth.
8. **iodine** (Y uh DYN): a liquid medicine that is used to clean and disinfect wounds.
9. **hedge** (hehj): fence of bushes.

Your TURN

SUMMARIZING

You have already identified at least two conflicts. Re-read lines 92–93. What new conflict might keep Alfonso from getting what he wants? Fill in the blank below: Somebody (Alfonso) wants

_____

but _____

but _____

but _____

_____

(You can add more *buts* if you count more than three conflicts so far.)

Your TURN

CONFLICT

Underline the words in lines 114–117 that point to an internal conflict for Alfonso. What feeling(s) is he struggling with here?

_____

_____

_____

_____

Ernie looked through the hedge at the girl. "She's not the one who messed with Frostie and me," he said finally. "You
120 still want to borrow my bike?"

Alfonso couldn't believe his luck. What a brother! He promised to take Ernie's turn doing the dishes. Ernie headed home.

Alfonso came out from behind the hedge with Ernie's
125 bike.

Sandra waved and smiled. "Hi," she said.

"Hi," he said back. Alfonso told her that his bike was broken. He asked if she wanted to ride with him.

"Sounds good," she said, and jumped on the crossbar.
130 He started off slowly because she was heavier than he thought. But once he got going, it got easier. He pedaled smoothly, sometimes with only one hand on the handlebars. They rode up one street and down another. Whenever he ran over a bump, she screamed with delight. Once, when it
135 looked like they were going to crash, she put her hand over his. It felt like love.

Conflict Ladder

Think of the plot of "Broken Chain" as a ladder. Each conflict that Alfonso faces is a step on a ladder. In the diagram below, some of the steps tell what the conflict is. Others give clues about the conflict. Identify the conflict Alfonso faces at every step up the ladder. To the right of each conflict, circle *Internal or External*. Between steps, jot down what happens between conflicts. At the top of the ladder, sketch the outcome: What does Alfonso finally get for all his struggling?

OUTCOME:

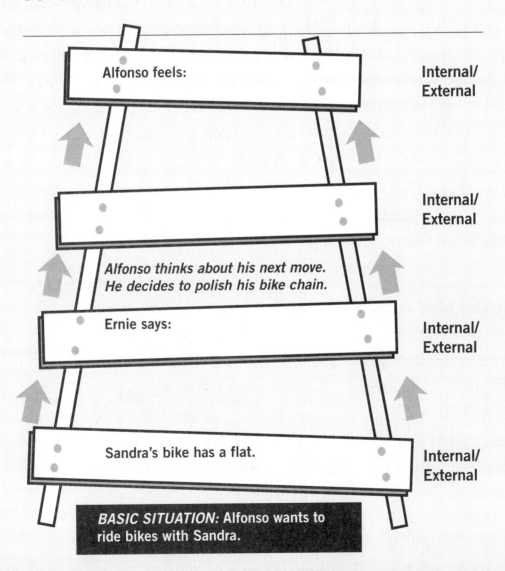

Alfonso feels:

Internal/
External

Internal/
External

Alfonso thinks about his next move. He decides to polish his bike chain.

Ernie says:

Internal/
External

Sandra's bike has a flat.

Internal/
External

BASIC SITUATION: Alfonso wants to ride bikes with Sandra.

Road Warriors, Listen Up: Some Rules for Streetwise Biking

Reading Skill: Analyzing Proposition and Support

Writers sometimes want to persuade their readers to agree with them. To do this, a writer may begin with a **proposition,** which is an important idea or opinion. Then, the writer will **support** the proposition with **reasons.** Strong reasons make the writer's proposition convincing.

Let's say that your friend wants to adopt a dog or a cat. You tell her that in your opinion, she should get a cat. When she asks why, you say that cats are very clean. You also point out that she wouldn't have to spend money on a leash. You could write down your proposition and reasons this way.

Proposition: You should get a cat as a pet.

1. Reason: Cats are very clean.

2. Reason: You don't have to buy a leash.

Into the Article

If you've ever ridden a bicycle on a busy street, you know it can be dangerous. You share the road with speeding fire engines and police cars. Sports cars and SUVs zip in and out of lanes. Giant trucks with eighteen wheels block your path—and your view. Everyone's in a hurry. How can you stay safe? Read the following article to learn one writer's opinion.

Road Warriors, Listen Up: Some Rules for Streetwise Biking

Based on the Article by

Madeline Travers Hovland

Here's
HOW

**PROPOSITION
AND SUPPORT**

The writer gets to her point quickly. She says in the first paragraph (lines 1-3) that if you want to be safe on your bike, you have to follow some basic rules. This must be the writer's proposition.

Here's
HOW

**PROPOSITION
AND SUPPORT**

In paragraph 2 (lines 4-8), the writer gives a reason to support her proposition. She says that not following safety rules could land you in the hospital—or the grave. That's pretty convincing!

Your
TURN

**PROPOSITION
AND SUPPORT**

In lines 24–28, underline two reasons the writer gives to support her proposition.

1 **W**hen you ride a bike, you have less protection than anyone else in a moving vehicle.[1] To ride a bike safely you've got to know and follow the rules of the road.

The results of not following bike-safety rules can be
5 painful, if not fatal.[2] Every year in the United States there are about eight hundred deaths due to bike accidents. More than half a million people end up in emergency rooms because of bike injuries.

Wear a bike helmet, even for a short ride. A helmet that
10 meets safety standards may be expensive, but your brain is worth the money. Bike helmets can reduce head injuries by as much as 80 percent.

Never ride wearing headphones. If you carry a cell phone or a pager, pull off the road to make a call or check your
15 beeper.

Obey all traffic signs and signals—these are for everyone on the road, not just cars. Ride in the same direction as all other traffic, not against it. Pedestrians[3] always have the right of way,[4] both on the sidewalk and in the street.

20 Watch for and steer around potholes, bumps, gravel, piles of leaves, and grates covering storm drains. Use hand signals to warn drivers when you're turning. When you're not making a hand signal, keep both hands on your handlebars.

Safe biking is great practice for driving a car. Even when
25 you're old enough to drive a car, however, you may still go biking. It's fun, it's a cheap way to travel, and it's great exercise. Whatever your age, always follow the rules for roadwise biking. The life you save may be your own!

---

1. **vehicle** (VEE uh kuhl): means of transportation, such as a car, bus, or truck.
2. **fatal** (FAY tuhl): causing death.
3. **pedestrians** (puh DEHS tree uhnz): walker; person moving around on foot.
4. **right of way:** right to move or go forward first.

Proposition and Support

Writers often want to persuade you to agree with them. The **proposition** is the most important point the writer makes about a subject. The writer then gives **reasons** that **support** the proposition. In the chart below, read the proposition the author of the article makes. Then, after re-reading the article, write one supporting reason in each box with an arrow. One has been done for you.

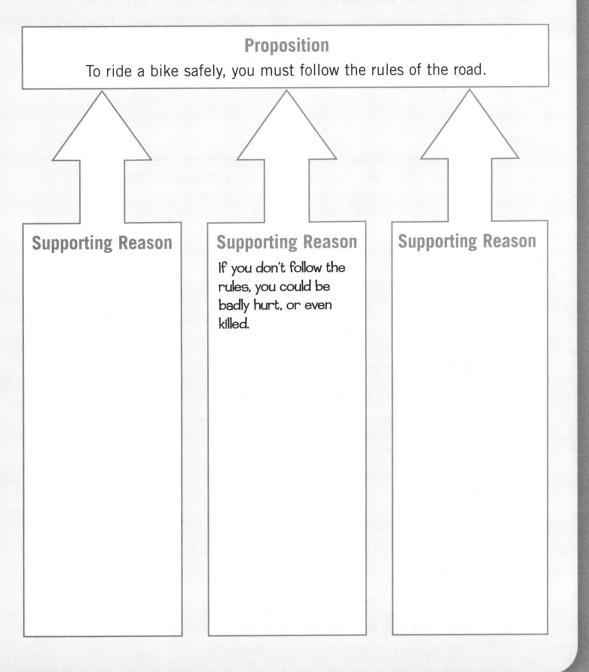

Proposition
To ride a bike safely, you must follow the rules of the road.

Supporting Reason

Supporting Reason

If you don't follow the rules, you could be badly hurt, or even killed.

Supporting Reason

The Landlady

Literary Focus: Foreshadowing

"Uh-oh. What's under the bed?" "Is he going to look under the bed?" A good suspense writer has you wondering what's going to happen next. To heighten the suspense, a writer will use clues, or **foreshadowing,** to suggest events that will happen later in the story. These clues lead you to ask many questions. You can keep track of your reading with a chart like this one.

Clues from Story	My Questions About Clues	What Happens in Story
The hero thinks he hears a noise from under the bed.	What's under the bed? Is he going to look under the bed?	He looks. Phew. It's just a black cat sleeping under the bed.

Reading Skill: Making Predictions

When you try to guess what will happen next, you are **making a prediction.** Don't worry if your prediction isn't correct. After all, if you could guess everything that happens in a story before it happens, you'd get bored. Clever writers will often surprise you.

Into the Story

Have you ever seen the movie *Willy Wonka and the Chocolate Factory?* That movie is based on a book by Roald Dahl. This author also wrote many stories for adults, including the one adapted here for you. In "The Landlady," Dahl has left many clever clues for you to figure out.

The Landlady

BASED ON THE STORY BY
Roald Dahl

1   **B**illy Weaver arrived in the town of Bath on business. He had traveled from London on the slow afternoon train. By the time he got to Bath, it was about nine o'clock in the evening. The air was <u>deadly</u> cold. Billy had never

5   been to Bath before. He didn't know anyone there. But Mr. Greenslade at the head office in London had told him it was a great town.

    Billy went to find a place to stay. He saw a sign in a window of a house. The sign said "Bed and Breakfast." Billy

10 went right up and looked through the window into the room. The first thing he saw was a bright fire burning in the fireplace. A cute little dog was curled up asleep on the carpet in front of the fire. The room itself was filled with pleasant furniture. Billy saw a large parrot in a cage in the corner of

15 the room. All in all, it looked like it would be a pretty decent place to stay. However, Billy decided he would walk on and take a look at some other places before making up his mind.

    And now a <u>strange</u> thing happened to him. He was stepping back and turning away from the window when his

20 eye was caught in the <u>strangest</u> way by the small sign that was there. BED AND BREAKFAST, it said. Each word was <u>like a large</u> black eye staring <u>at him</u> through the glass. The sign <u>held him</u>. It <u>forced him to stay</u> where he was. The next thing Billy knew, he was moving to the front door of the house and

25 reaching for the doorbell.

    He didn't even have time to take his finger from the bell button when the door swung open. A woman was standing there. She was about forty-five or fifty years old. The moment she saw him, she gave him a warm, welcoming smile.

30   "My dear boy," she said, "why don't you come in out of the cold?"

    Billy asked, "How much do you charge?"

    "Five and sixpence a night, including breakfast," the woman answered.

35   It was very cheap. It was less than half of what he had been willing to pay.

    "That's fine," Billy said. "I would like very much to stay here."

    "I knew you would. Do come in."

40   She seemed terribly nice. She looked exactly like the mother of one's best school friend. Billy took off his hat and stepped inside.

    "We have it *all* to ourselves," she said. She smiled at him over her shoulder as she led the way upstairs. "You see, it

45 isn't very often I have the pleasure of taking a visitor into my little nest."

    The lady seems a little crazy, Billy told himself. But for such a great price, who cares about that? "I would think many people would want to stay here," he said politely.

50   "Oh, yes, my dear. But the trouble is that I'm a bit picky. I'm always ready, though, in case the right young man comes along. It's such a pleasure to open the door and see someone standing there who is *exactly* right." She was halfway up the stairs when she turned around. She smiled and added, "Like

55 you."

    On the second floor, she said to him, "This floor is mine."

    They climbed up another flight. "And this one is all yours," she said. "Here's your room. I do hope you like it."

THE LANDLADY   **15**

MAKING PREDICTIONS

Hmmm. I didn't predict that Billy would choose to stay here. But I can see why he decided to. It's cold outside, and the Bed and Breakfast is cozy and cheap.

Your TURN

VOCABULARY

The word *terribly* usually means "fearfully" or "dreadfully." In line 40, however, *terribly* means something else. What does it mean?

_____

_____

Why do you think the writer chose the word *terribly*?

_____

_____

_____

FORESHADOWING

I think it's strange that the landlady doesn't have any other visitors. She's so eager to have Billy. It's weird that she says he's "exactly right" (line 53).

**MAKING
PREDICTIONS**

Re-read lines 66–70. Do
you think Billy is right that
he has nothing to worry
about? Explain your answer
below.

_____

_____

_____

_____

FORESHADOWING

Huh? The dog doesn't get up
to greet Billy (lines 73-74)?
That's odd. My dog always
notices people coming into
the room.

**MAKING
PREDICTIONS**

Re-read lines 84–89. Why
do you think the names
Gregory Temple and
Christopher Mulholland
sound familiar to Billy?

_____

_____

_____

"Thank you," Billy said. He noticed that the bedspread
had been taken off the bed, making it ready for someone to
get in.

"I'll leave you now so that you can unpack. But before
you go to bed, would you come downstairs and sign the
guest book? Everyone has to do that. That's the rule." She
said goodbye and went quickly out of the room.

Now, the fact that his landlady seemed to be a little odd
didn't worry Billy in the least. After all, not only was she
harmless—but she was also obviously a kind and generous
soul. He guessed that she had probably lost a son in the war
and had never gotten over it.

So, after unpacking his suitcase, Billy went downstairs. He
entered the living room. His landlady wasn't there, but the
fire was glowing in the fireplace. The little dog was sleeping
soundly in front of it. The room was so warm and cozy. I'm a
lucky guy, he thought.

He found the guest book lying open on the piano. He took
out his pen and wrote down his name and address. There
were only two other entries above his on the page. One was a
Christopher Mulholland. The other was a Gregory W. Temple.

That's funny, he thought suddenly. Christopher
Mulholland. Now where on earth had he heard that rather
unusual name before? He looked at the book again. Now that
he thought about it, the second name also seemed familiar.

"Gregory Temple?" he said aloud, searching his memory.
"Christopher Mulholland? . . ."

"Such charming boys," a voice behind him answered.
Billy turned and saw his landlady. She was coming into the
room carrying a large silver tea tray in her hands.

"They sound somehow familiar," he said.

90   "They do? How interesting."

Once more, Billy glanced down at the book. This time he noticed the dates. "Look here. This last entry is over two years old."

"It is?"

95   "Yes, indeed. And Christopher Mulholland's is nearly a year before that—more than three years ago."

"Dear me," she said, shaking her head. "I would never have thought it. Time flies."

Billy stared at the book. "Now wait a minute," he said.
100 "Wait just a minute. Mulholland . . . Christopher Mulholland . . . wasn't that the name of the boy who was taking a trip, and then all of a sudden . . ."

"Milk?" she said. "And sugar?"

"Yes, please. And then all of a sudden . . ."

105   "Come on. Your tea's all ready for you," she patted the empty place beside her on the sofa. She sat there smiling at Billy and waiting for him.

He crossed the room slowly and sat down on the edge of the sofa. She placed his teacup on the table in front of him.

110   "There we are," she said. "How nice and cozy this is, isn't it?"

Billy started sipping his tea. She did the same. For half a minute or so, neither of them spoke. But Billy knew she was looking at him. Now and again, he smelled something
115 strange coming from her direction. It was not the least unpleasant, and it reminded him of something. Pickled walnuts? Leather? Or was it a hospital?

"I guess Mr. Mulholland left recently," Billy said. He was still trying to figure out where he had heard the two names.
120 He was positive now that he had seen them in the newspapers—in the headlines.

Your TURN

MAKING PREDICTIONS

On the previous page you made a prediction about why the names sound familiar to Billy. Now, re-read lines 100–107. Then, decide if you want to keep your original prediction or revise it. Explain your answer below.

_____

_____

_____

_____

Your TURN

FORESHADOWING

After reading lines 118–121, you probably have a question. Write your question below.

_____

_____

_____

_____

_____

Your TURN

FORESHADOWING

Notice that the landlady uses the present tense (*is*) in lines 122-123. Underline the verbs in lines 129–132. What verb tense does the landlady use here?

_____

_____

Why is this shift from *is* to *was* important?

_____

_____

_____

_____

_____

_____

Here's HOW

MAKING PREDICTIONS

I knew something was wrong with that dog! I picked up on the foreshadowing clues, but I didn't predict that the landlady stuffed her animals. Yikes! In line 132, the landlady seems to know a lot about Mr. Temple's skin. Maybe she stuffed him, too!

"Left?" she said. "But, my dear boy, he never left. He's still here. Mr. Temple is also here. They're on the fourth floor, both of them together."

125   Billy set his cup down slowly on the table and stared at the landlady. She put out one of her white hands and patted him on the knee. "How old are you, my dear?" she asked.

    "Seventeen."

    "Seventeen!" she cried. "Oh, it's the perfect age! Mr.
130 Mulholland was also seventeen. Mr. Temple, of course, was a little older. He was actually twenty-eight. I would never have guessed it unless he told me. His skin was *just* like a baby's."

    Billy picked up his teacup and took another sip of his tea. He set down the teacup and waited for her to say something
135 else. He sat there staring straight ahead of him.

    "That parrot," he said at last. "You know something? It had me completely fooled when I first saw it through the window. I could have sworn it was alive."

    "Not anymore."

140   "It doesn't look dead at all," he said. "Who did it?"

    "I did."

    "*You* did?"

    "Of course," she said. "And have you met my little Basil as well?" She nodded toward the dog curled up so
145 comfortably in front of the fire. Billy looked at it. And suddenly he realized that all the time this animal had been just as dead as the parrot. She explained, "I stuff all my little pets myself when they pass away. Will you have another cup of tea?"

150   "No, thank you," Billy said. The tea tasted of bitter almonds. He didn't really like it.

    "I'm glad you signed the book. Because later on, if I happen to forget what you were called, then I could always

come down here and look it up. I still do that almost every
155 day with Mr. Mulholland and Mr. . . . Mr. . . ."

"Temple," Billy said. "Gregory Temple. Excuse my asking,
but haven't there been any other guests here except them in
the last two or three years?"

She looked up at him and gave him another gentle little
160 smile.

"No, my dear," she said. "Only you."

Your
TURN

MAKING
PREDICTIONS

What do you think will
happen now? Support
your prediction with
foreshadowing clues from
the story.

Foreshadowing: Chart Your Reading

Roald Dahl is famous for writing suspenseful stories full of dark humor. When most readers finish one of his stories, they like to read it again. They check to see if he dropped any clues that should have helped them predict how the story was going. These clues planted in the story are called **foreshadowing.** Foreshadowing clues lead you to ask many questions.

What kinds of questions did you ask yourself when you were reading "The Landlady"? Chart your reading below. In the first column, read the foreshadowing clues. In the second column, write the questions that were in your mind when you read each clue in the story. In the third column, write what happens in the story to answer your question. The first row has been filled in for you.

Foreshadowing Clues	My Questions	What Happens in Story
1. The landlady doesn't have any other visitors. (lines 43–55)	Why doesn't she have any visitors when she seems so lonely and eager to have Billy?	It turns out she's only had three visitors. The first two visitors never left!
2. The dog never moves. (lines 12–13; lines 73–74)		
3. The two names in the guest book sound familiar to Billy. (lines 80–90)		

Foreshadowing: Picture the Clues

When Billy Weaver first looks into the window of the landlady's Bed and Breakfast, he sees a cozy (comfortable) living room. The writer describes the room in **lines 8–16.** Later in the story, Billy goes down to the living room to sign the guest book. Again, he notes how cozy the room seems. The narrator describes the scene in **lines 71–75.** The rest of the story takes place in this room while Billy and the landlady talk.

This living room is full of **foreshadowing clues**! Look over the descriptions of the living room. Then, draw a picture of the room in the space below. Finally, draw arrows to the foreshadowing clues and label them. You can make your drawing realistic, or you can make it free-floating like the picture of the teacup below.

Clue: The tea tastes like bitter almonds.

Barbara Frietchie

Literary Focus: A Character's Character

We read about characters in stories and poems. But each of us carries "character" inside of ourselves, too. In this sense, **character** means "a person's real nature or personality."

Reading Skill: Paraphrasing

Paraphrasing means retelling a piece of writing in your own words. A summary tells only the most important ideas. A paraphrase retells *all* the ideas. For this reason, a paraphrase is usually longer than a summary. You might paraphrase the first four lines of "Barbara Frietchie" like this.

Whittier's Words	My Words
Up from the meadows rich with corn, Clear in the cool September morn, The clustered spires of Frederick stand Green-walled by the hills of Maryland.	On a cool September morning, the church steeples of Frederick stand out clearly above the cornfields. The church steeples are surrounded by the green hills of Maryland.

Into the Poem

This poem is set in 1862, during the American Civil War. On September 6, Southern troops marched into the town of Frederick, Maryland. Generals Robert E. Lee and Stonewall Jackson led them. Because Maryland was a slave slate, the Southern forces expected a warm welcome. However, the people of Frederick were loyal to the Union. Not all of the people had the courage to display the Union flag. However, Barbara Frietchie did.

Barbara Frietchie

John Greenleaf Whittier

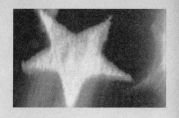

VOCABULARY

To find out what the word *famished* (line 8) means, I looked it up in a dictionary. The entry for *famished* says "suffering from lack of food." This makes sense. The fruit trees looked like the garden of Eden to the rebels. They must have been hungry.

Here's
HOW

PARAPHRASE

Lines 13–16 make up a single sentence, but it's a hard one. I'll paraphrase it to make sure I understand what it means. *Forty flags with stars and stripes flew in the morning breeze. But by noon, not a single one remained.*

Your
TURN

PARAPHRASE

In your own words, tell what happens in lines 17–22:

_____

_____

_____

_____

1   **U**p from the meadows rich with corn,
Clear in the cool September morn,

The clustered spires[1] of Frederick stand
Green-walled by the hills of Maryland.

5   Round about them orchards sweep,
Apple and peach tree fruited deep,

Fair as the garden of the Lord
To the eyes of the famished rebel horde,[2]

On that pleasant morn of the early fall
10 When Lee marched over the mountain wall;

Over the mountains winding down,
Horse and foot, into Frederick town.

Forty flags with their silver stars,
Forty flags with their crimson bars,

15 Flapped in the morning wind: the sun
Of noon looked down, and saw not one.

Up rose old Barbara Frietchie then,
Bowed with her fourscore years and ten;[3]

Bravest of all in Frederick town,
20 She took up the flag the men hauled down

---

1. **spires:** steeples.
2. **horde:** moving crowd.
3. **fourscore years and ten:** ninety years (a score = twenty years; 4 × 20 = 80; 80 + 10 = 90.

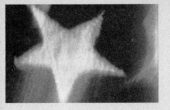

In her attic window the staff[4] she set,
To show that one heart was loyal yet.

Up the street came the rebel tread,[5]
Stonewall Jackson riding ahead.

25 Under his slouched hat[6] left and right
He glanced; the old flag met his sight.

"Halt!"—the dust-brown ranks stood fast.
"Fire!"—out blazed the rifle blast.

It shivered the window, pane and sash;[7]
30 It rent the banner with seam and gash.

Quick, as it fell, from the broken staff
Dame Barbara snatched the silken scarf.

She leaned far out on the windowsill,
And shook it forth with a royal will.

35 "Shoot, if you must, this old gray head,
But spare your country's flag," she said.

A shade of sadness, a blush of shame,
Over the face of the leader came;

The nobler nature within him stirred
40 To life at that woman's deed and word;

Here's HOW

A CHARACTER'S CHARACTER

I guess flying a flag was a way of saying which side you were on. It must have taken courage for Barbara Frietchie to tell the rebel soldiers she was on the Union side. She had guts!

Your TURN

VOCABULARY

The word *rent* in line 30 can mean "to pay money for a place to live" or "to rip or tear." Underline the meaning the word has here.

Your TURN

PARAPHRASE

Write lines 39–40 in your own words.

_____

_____

_____

_____

_____

---

4. **staff:** pole.
5. **tread:** footsteps; sound of marching feet.
6. **slouched hat:** a soft hat with a broad, drooping brim.
7. **pane and sash:** window glass and frame.

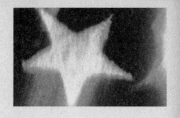

Here's
HOW

PARAPHRASE

I think lines 43–46 are saying this: *All day long, the sound of marching rebels could be heard in the streets of Frederick. And all day long, the flag flew over the rebels' heads.*

Your
TURN

A CHARACTER'S CHARACTER

Why does the speaker, who seems loyal to the Union, ask us to shed a tear for Stonewall Jackson, a rebel leader (lines 53–54)? How did Jackson earn the speaker's respect?

_____

_____

Your
TURN

PARAPHRASE

Paraphrase lines 55–60. Note that in these lines the speaker talks directly to the Union flag.

_____

_____

_____

_____

"Who touches a hair of yon[8] gray head
Dies like a dog! March on!" he said.

All day long through Frederick street
Sounded the tread of marching feet:

45 All day long that free flag tossed
Over the heads of the rebel host.

Ever its torn folds rose and fell
On the loyal winds that loved it well;

And through the hill gaps sunset light
50 Shone over it with a warm good night.

Barbara Frietchie's work is o'er,
And the Rebel rides on his raids no more.

Honor to her! and let a tear
Fall, for her sake, on Stonewall's bier.[9]

55 Over Barbara Frietchie's grave,
Flag of Freedom and Union, wave!

Peace and order and beauty draw
Round thy symbol of light and law;

And ever the stars above look down
60 On thy stars below in Frederick town!

---

8. **yon:** yonder—over there.
9. **bier** (bihr): coffin and the platform on which it rests. Stonewall Jackson died in 1863 after being wounded in battle.

Paraphrase Organizer

Use the organizer below to put together a complete paraphrasing of "Barbara Frietchie." Use your responses from "Your Turn" activities to help fill in the organizer.

Lines 1–4	The church spires of Frederick rise up from the cornfields, clear in the September morning. The spires are surrounded by the green hills of Maryland.
Lines 5–12	
Lines 13–16	Forty flags with stars and stripes flew in the morning breeze. But by noon, not a single one remained.
Lines 17–22	
Lines 23–30	Stonewall Jackson rode in front of the rebel troops. From under his hat, he looked left and right. When he saw the old flag, he shouted "Halt!" and then, "Fire!" The troops shot at the flag, tearing it and shattering the window from which it was flying.
Lines 31–36	
Lines 37–42	
Lines 43–46	All day long, the sound of marching rebels could be heard in the streets of Frederick. And all day long, the flag flew over the rebels' heads.
Lines 47–54	
Lines 55–60	Union Flag, I say to you:

Union Pacific Railroad Poster
and Home, Sweet Soddie

Reading Skill: Compare and Contrast Texts

Two texts might have same subject, but they might treat these subjects very differently. If a text gives only one side of the subject, it is **biased.** If it gives many sides of the subject, it is **objective.**

Take a look at this well-known song.

Oh, give me a home

Where the buffalo roam

Where the deer and the antelope play

Where seldom is heard

A discouraging word

And the skies are not cloudy all day

The song doesn't tell about the dangers and hardships on the prairie. The song expresses only one point of view. Therefore, this text is **biased.**

Into the Article

In 1803, the United States bought land from France that doubled the size of the United States. Thousands of pioneers began heading west. When the government passed the Homestead Act of 1862, a pioneer settler could own up to 160 acres by living on it for five years. However, homesteaders faced many hardships. Of the thousands of families that homesteaded on the prairies, more than half failed and had to give up their land.

Union Pacific Railroad Poster

RICH FARMING LANDS!

ON THE LINE OF THE

Union Pacific Railroad!

Located in the GREAT CENTRAL BELT of POPULATION, COMMERCE and WEALTH, and adjoining the WORLD'S HIGHWAY from OCEAN TO OCEAN.

12,000,000 ACRES!

3,000,000 Acres in Central and Eastern Nebraska, in the Platte Valley, now for sale!

invite the attention of all parties seeking a HOME, to the

Home, Sweet Soddie

Based on the Article by

Flo Ota De Lange

RICH FARMING LANDS!

ON THE LINE OF THE

Union Pacific Railroad!

Located in the GREAT CENTRAL BELT of POPULATION, COMMERCE and WEALTH, and next to the WORLD'S HIGHWAY from OCEAN TO OCEAN.

12,000,000 ACRES!

3,000,000 Acres in Central and Eastern Nebraska, in the Platte Valley, now for sale!

We invite the attention of all parties seeking a HOME, to the LANDS offered for sale by this Company.

1   **The Huge Amount of Land** from which to choose means that everyone can have the location he wants. The land is suitable for any type of farming and the raising of farm animals.

5   **The Prices are Very Low.** The amount of land owned by the Company is so large that they are going to sell at the cheapest possible prices, ranging from $1.50 to $8.00 per acre.

The Terms of Payment are Easy. No payments for ten 10 years at six percent interest. A deduction of ten percent for cash.

The Location is Central, along the 41st parallel,[1] the favorite latitude[2] of America. The area does not have the long, cold winters of the Northern States. It does not have the 15 hot, unhealthy climate of the Southern States.

The Face of the Country is varied. There are hills and valleys, grain land and meadow, and rich land along the rivers. There are low cliffs and level prairies,[3] all covered with a thick growth of sweet nutritious grasses.

---

1. **parallel** (PAR uh lehl): imaginary line that circles the earth, always the same distance from the equator.
2. **latitude** (LAT uh TOOD): distance from the equator.
3. **prairies** (PREHR eez): level grasslands.

20   **The Soil** is a dark and fertile, with a small amount of lime.[4] There is no stone and gravel. The soil is well suited to grass, grain, and root crops.[5] The layer under the topsoil is usually light and soaks up water.

The Climate is mild and healthful. The air is dry and
25 pure. There is little disease and malaria[6] is unknown. The greatest amount of rain falls between March and October. The Winters are dry with little snow.

Wood for building is found along the streams.

The Title given the purchaser is final, with full rights. It
30 is free from any claims, and comes directly from the United States.

Soldiers of the Late War have the right to a Homestead of one hundred and sixty acres, within Railroad limits. This is equal to a reward of $400.

35 **Persons of Foreign Birth** also have a right to the benefits of the Free Homestead Law, when they say they intend to become a citizen of the United States. They may make this statement immediately on their arrival in this country.

40   Full information about land, prices, terms of sale, etc., along with pamphlets, circulars[7] and maps, may be obtained from the Agents of the Department, also the

"PIONEER."

A handsome Illustrated Paper, with maps, etc., and
45   containing the Homestead Law. Mailed free to all applicants.

Address

O. F. DAVIS,

Land Commissioner, U. P. R. R.

50 OMAHA, NEB.

---

4. lime: chalk in the soil.
5. root crops: what is grown underground, such as potatoes and carrots.
6. malaria (muh LEHR ee uh): a disease spread by mosquitoes.
7. circulars (SUR kyuh luhrz): advertisements; printed notices.

COMPARE AND CONTRAST TEXTS

Re-read lines 24–27. What does the poster say about the climate?

_____

_____

_____

COMPARE AND CONTRAST TEXTS

Do you think the poster gives a biased or an objective description of the land for sale?

_____

_____

_____

Here's
HOW

COMPARE AND CONTRAST TEXTS

I think the subject of this text is living on the land. This article may tell a different story about life on the prairie.

Your
TURN

COMPARE AND CONTRAST TEXTS

In the second paragraph (lines 5–15), underline one bad thing about living in a sod house.

Your
TURN

COMPARE AND CONTRAST TEXTS

In the third paragraph (lines 16–24), underline one good thing about living in a sod house.

Home, Sweet Soddie[1]

1 Here you are, a pioneer on the prairie, settled for your first night in your new Home Sweet Home. The first thing you notice is that it is absolutely dark at night in your new home built of sod.

5 **Thousands of Worms**

So when the first crack of dawn[2] comes, you're anxious to see your new world. But what's that? It looks like the ceiling above your head is moving. No, it couldn't be. Look again. Now it looks like the wall is moving too. You shut your

10 eyes. While you are lying there with your eyes squeezed tightly shut, your mother yells, "This place is alive with worms!" You open your eyes and, sure enough, there are worms hanging from the ceiling. There arre worms waving at you from the walls. What's that all over the floor? More

15 worms—Hundreds—no, thousands of worms!

Houses Built of Soil

There are few trees on a prairie, so the pioneers built their first houses out of sod[3] bricks. The bricks were cut from the top layer of soil. A sod brick included all the

20 grasses and roots growing in the dirt. Sod houses were strong and long lasting because of the thick root system in the prairie grassland. They were cool in summer and warm in winter. They protected the pioneers from tornadoes, wind, and fire.

25 **No Sense Cleaning It!**

What were the disadvantages of a sod house? Sod is hard-packed dirt. As the sod dried out, loose dirt fell off the walls and ceiling. Dirt got into everything. It was almost impossible to keep the house clean. Sod wasn't waterproof. When it

---

1. **Soddie:** sod house.
2. **crack of dawn:** the time when the sun begins to rise.
3. **sod**: grass-covered ground.

30 rained, water ran down the roots in the sod bricks, right
through the ceiling. Everything in the room was soaked and
the floor was turned to mud. The roof could leak for days.
People sometimes had to use boots and umbrellas indoors
while the sun was shining brightly outside!

35 **Bugs and Weather**

Other difficulties faced by a pioneer on the prairie
included fleas, flies, mosquitoes, moths, bedbugs, field
mice, rattlesnakes, and grasshoppers. The fleas and bedbugs
come crawling out of the sod walls at night. So every

40 morning you have to take your bitten self and your infested
bedding out-of-doors and pick off all those bugs. Then you
head back inside with chicken feathers dipped in kerosene[4]
to paint every crack and every crevice[5] in every bit of that
sod ceiling, wall, and floor.

45 Other hazards were tornadoes, floods, hail, blizzards,[6]
prairie fires, dust storms, and drought.[7] In summer the
ground baked hard as brick, and in winter it froze hard as
iron. The wind blew constantly, and water was as scarce as
hens' teeth.[8]

50 **Blizzards of Grasshoppers**

You may know about blizzards of snow. But what about a
blizzard of grasshoppers—so many millions of grasshoppers
that they block out the sun and strip a farm bare in a matter
of hours? Did you know that grasshoppers can eat almost

55 everything, including fences, plough handles, and that
bedding that you just picked clean of fleas and bedbugs? If a
pioneer family had dug 150 feet down for a well—the height
of a thirteen-story building—grasshoppers falling into it
could spoil the water for weeks. Grasshoppers could even

---

4. **kerosene** (KEHR uh seen): colorless oil used in lamps and stoves.
5. **crevice** (KREV ihs): narrow split or crack.
6. **blizzards** (BLIHZ uhrdz): cold, snowy storm.
7. **drought** (drowt): no rain.
8. **scarce as hen's teeth:** very little or nothing. Hens don't have teeth.

Your TURN

VOCABULARY

The word *infested* (line 40) means "full of" or "overrun in large numbers." Re-read lines 36–44 and underline the words that help define *infested*.

Here's HOW

VOCABULARY

I think the word *hazards* (line 45) means "dangers." All the things named in the same sentence as the word *hazards* are really dangerous.

Your TURN

COMPARE AND CONTRAST TEXTS

Why do you think the grasshopper problem was not mentioned in the poster?

_____

_____

_____

60 stop a Union Pacific Railroad train from running. Their bodies piled up to six inches deep on the tracks and were like grease on the rails. A train's wheels would spin but not move.

No Warranties

Homesteading on the prairie was hard work, and there
65 were no warranties—guarantees or promises—on claimed land. The buyers had to take all the risks upon themselves. The term for this arrangement is *caveat emptor*[9]—"let the buyer beware." So what can you do but sweep all that dirt out the front door and back onto the prairie? What else can
70 happen, after all?

---

9. **caveat emptor** (KAY vee AT EHMP TAWR).

Compare and Contrast Texts

When you **compare and contrast texts,** you look at ways they are alike and ways they are different. In the left-hand column of the chart below are questions about the two texts in this selection. Answer the questions for each of the texts. Some of the questions have been answered for you.

Questions	Union Pacific Poster	Home, Sweet Soddie
What is the subject?	farmland	life on the prairie
What is each writer's purpose?	the writer wants people to buy land	
In your opinion, is the text *biased* or *objective*?		biased
Give at least two details that show bias— how the writer feels about the subject.	the words "rich farming lands" and "healthful climate"	
Does this text make you want to live on the prairie?		

Mrs. Flowers

Literary Focus: A Character's Influence

The word *influence* comes from the Latin word *influere,* meaning "to flow into." When someone **influences** you, it's as if their ideas and feelings flow into you. Who has had the greatest influence on *you*?

In this autobiographical story, a woman named Mrs. Flowers has an important influence on a young girl named Marguerite. As you read, think about how Mrs. Flowers changes Marguerite's life.

INFLUENCES

Mrs. Flowers ⟶ Marguerite

Reading Skill: Determining the Main Idea

The **main idea** is the most important idea in a story. Often the writer tells you the main idea. Sometimes it is up to you to figure it out. You have to use details in the story to find out what larger—or main—idea the writer is getting at. Keeping track of key details will help you determine the main idea.

Into the Story

When the author was a little girl, she and her brother went to live with their grandmother, who owned a general store. A year before meeting Mrs. Flowers, the author had been attacked by a family friend. The pain she felt was so deep that she had stopped speaking altogether.

Mrs. Flowers

FROM I Know Why the Caged Bird Sings

Based on the Autobiography by
Maya Angelou

1   For almost a year, I hung around the house, the Store, the school, and the church, sad and unhappy. I felt like an old biscuit, one that nobody wanted. Then I met the lady who saved me from my deep sadness.

5   Mrs. Bertha Flowers was a gentlewoman.[1] She showed me the best that any person can be.

I'll never forget that special summer afternoon when she stopped at the Store to buy groceries. Another Negro woman her age would have carried her own groceries

10 home. But Momma said, "Sister Flowers, I'll send Bailey[2] up to your house with these things."

Mrs. Flowers smiled her slow, beautiful smile that made me feel warm and loved. "Thank you, Mrs. Henderson," she said. "I'd prefer Marguerite, though." My name was beautiful

15 when she said it. "I've been meaning to talk to her." Momma and Mrs. Flowers gave each other a grown-up look.

Mrs. Flowers walked in front along the rocky path. The thin fabric of her flowered dress floated gently in the breeze. She said, without turning her head, "I hear you're doing very

20 good schoolwork, Marguerite. But it's all written work. The teachers say that you do not talk." The path became wider here. We could walk together. I stayed back.

"Come and walk along with me, Marguerite." I had to give in and walk beside her. She said my name so nicely.

25   "Now no one is going to make you talk," said Mrs. Flowers. "But keep in mind, it is only people who talk to one another. It is the one thing that makes us different from animals." That was a new idea to me. I would need time to think about it.

---

1. **gentlewoman:** a woman who is polite, considerate, and dignified.
2. Bailey is the author's younger brother.

Excerpt (retitled "Mrs. Flowers") adapted from *I Know Why the Caged Bird Sings* by Maya Angelou. Copyright © 1969 and renewed © 1997 by Maya Angelou. For online information about other Random House, Inc. books and authors, see the Internet Web site at http://www.randomhouse.com. Retold by Holt, Rinehart and Winston. Reproduced by permission of **Random House, Inc.**

30 "Your grandmother says you read a lot. That's good, but not good enough. Words need a person's voice to fill them with meaning."

I memorized the part about a person's voice filling words with meaning. It seemed so true.

35 Mrs. Flowers said she was going to give me some books. I was to take good care of them. I was to read them aloud. I was to read each sentence in as many different ways as possible.

The sweet smell of vanilla met us as she opened the 40 door of her house.

"I made tea cookies this morning. I planned to invite you for cookies and lemonade. I wanted to talk with you."

She took the grocery bags from me and disappeared through the kitchen door. I looked around the room.
45 Photographs looked down from the walls. The white, freshly ironed curtains moved with the wind. I wanted to gather up the whole room and take it to Bailey. He would help me figure it out.

"Have a seat, Marguerite. Over there by the table." She
50 carried a plate covered with a tea towel. She said she had not baked cookies for a long time. I was sure her cookies would be perfect, just as she was perfect.

The cookies were flat and round. They were a light brown on the edges, and butter-yellow in the center. With
55 the cold lemonade they were all I ever wanted to eat. I remembered my manners and took little bites off the edges. She said she had made them just for me, and she had some left in the kitchen. I could take these home to my brother. So I pushed one whole cookie in my mouth. I
60 wanted to keep it there. Not swallow it. It was a dream come true.

TURN

A CHARACTER'S INFLUENCE

Re-read lines 72–75. What effect does Mrs. Flowers's reading aloud have on Marguerite? What does Marguerite realize at this point?

_____

_____

Your

TURN

MAIN IDEA

In lines 88–92, underline the words that show the effect Mrs. Flowers has on Marguerite. Then, tell what you think is the main idea in this story.

_____

_____

As I ate, Mrs. Flowers began the first of "my lessons in living." She said that I must not put up with ignorance. I must be understanding of illiteracy.[3] I was to understand that
65 people who were not able to go to school sometimes knew more than college professors. She wanted me to listen carefully when all people spoke. I was to listen for plain sense[4] and wise words.

I finished the cookies. She brought a thick, small book
70 from the bookcase. I had already read *A Tale of Two Cities*. She opened the first page and began to read.

"It was the best of times, it was the worst of times. . . ." Her voice seemed to sing the words. I wanted to look at those pages. Were the words the same that I had read? Or
75 were they changed into music?

"How do you like that?"

It came to me that she expected me to answer her question. The sweet vanilla taste was still on my tongue. Her reading was a wonder in my ears. I had to speak.
80 I said, "Yes, ma'am." That was all I could say.

"Take this book of poems and memorize one for me. Next time you pay me a visit, I want you to recite."[5]

On that first day, I ran down the hill and I didn't stop running until I reached the Store.
85 I was liked. What a difference it made. I was respected. Not as Mrs. Henderson's grandchild or Bailey's sister but for just being me. Marguerite Johnson.

I did not ask why Mrs. Flowers began to pay attention to me. It did not occur to me that Momma might have asked
90 her to talk to me. All I cared about was that Mrs. Flowers made tea cookies for me. She read to me from her favorite book. It was enough. It proved that she liked me.

---

3. **illiteracy** (ih LIHT uhr uh see): lack of ability to read; lack of learning or education.
4. **sense** (sehns): meaning.
5. **recite** (rih SYT): say from memory.

A Character's Influence

Imagine you are Marguerite from the story. You want to present an award to Mrs. Flowers for being the person who has had the most and best influence on your life. In the space below, write about your admiration and gratitude. Why do you like Mrs. Flowers so much? Why are you thankful? To be as specific as possible, look back to the story for details.

Influence Award

To: Mrs. Flowers

In admiration and gratitude for

_____

_____

_____

_____

_____

_____

_____

Fast, Strong, and Friendly Too

Reading Skill: Comparison and Contrast

When writers want to describe two or more things, they
sometimes use **comparison and contrast.** When you compare,
you look at how things are similar. When you contrast, you
note how things are different. Think about two dogs you may
have known. You could use a Venn diagram to compare
these two dogs.

Rover   Brownie

different   **alike**   **different**

Coat: Black   Habits: Coat: Brown
Ears: One flops down   barks a lot   Ears: Floppy
Size: Small   Size: Medium
Habits: Chases cars.   Habits: Sleeps on my bed.

Into the Article

People in the far north have depended upon huskies for
more than 1,000 years. These hearty dogs stand about two
feet high and weigh between forty and fifty pounds. They
have a thick outer coat of fur, as well as an undercoat. The
undercoat allows huskies to sleep outside in temperatures as
low as −70 degrees Fahrenheit! Huskies are often used to
pull sleds across snow and ice. In the early 1900s, huskies
helped explorers reach the North and South Poles. They also
helped deliver mail to remote communities in Alaska and
Canada.

Fast, Strong, and Friendly Too

Based on the Article by

Flo Ota De Lange

Here's
HOW

COMPARING AND
CONTRASTING

The first paragraph names
some ways that all huskies
are alike: They are work
dogs, they are from the far
north, and they are used to
pull sleds.

Your
TURN

COMPARING AND
CONTRASTING

In lines 10–14, underline
one detail about the
Samoyed that tells what
makes it different from the
other dogs.

Your
TURN

VOCABULARY

What do you think the word
uncanny means in line 16?
Check your meaning in a
dictionary.

1   **H**uskies are the working dogs of the Arctic[1] They are
often used as sled dogs. Types of this dog include the
Siberian husky, the Samoyed[2], and the Alaskan malamute[3].

Siberian huskies were bred[4] originally by the Chukchi[5]
5   people of Siberia. The Chukchi trained them to run quickly
over great distances. Siberian huskies have won most of the
dog-team-racing titles in Alaska. Siberian huskies are
particularly good with children—Chukchi children were
encouraged to play with the dogs.

10   The Samoyed is most closely related to the first dogs.
There are no wolf or fox bloodlines[6] in the Samoyed breed.
For hundreds of years, the Samoyed has been bred true in the
huge stretches of central Siberia. There they were sled dogs,
reindeer guards, and household companions.

15   The Samoyed is a wonderful companion, with an almost
uncanny understanding of people. Intelligent and good-
natured; they always protect and never harm their human
families. Some people consider Samoyeds to be the most
beautiful of all dogs.

20   Alaskan malamutes are the largest of the sled dogs,
standing some two feet high. These dogs have remarkable
endurance[7] and courage. They were bred in Alaska by
people called Mahlemuts, or Malemutes. The Alaskan
malamutes are known for their loyalty, understanding, and
25   intelligence.

---

1. **Arctic** (AHRK tihk): region near the North Pole.
2. **Samoyed** (SAM uh YEHD).
3. **malamute** (MAL uh MYOOT).
4. **bred:** raised to produce young.
5. **Chukchi** (CHUK chee).
6. **bloodlines:** direct lines of ancestors that are all the same type.
7. **endurance** (ehn DUR uhns): the power and strength to last.

Compare-and-Contrast Chart

When you **compare,** you tell how things are alike. When you **contrast,** you tell how they are different. In the left-hand column of the chart below are the names of the three types of dogs in the article, "Fast, Strong, and Friendly Too." In the middle column are listed the places where these dogs were bred. In the right-hand column are some of the special qualities of these dogs. See if you can fill in the empty spaces in the chart. Look back through the article for help.

Breed of Dog	Where Bred	Special Qualitites
Siberian husky		1. good sled dogs 2. 3.
Samoyed	Siberia	1. sled dogs 2. 3. beautiful
Alaskan malamute	Alaska	1. 2. 3.

Destination: Mars

Reading Skill: Text Structure: Magazines

Do you like to read about movie stars? Sports? Current events? No matter what you are interested in, you can probably find a **magazine** about it.

Magazines are divided into parts that help you know what's inside.

The cover. The art and big words on a magazine's cover tell you what the main articles are. Smaller words might tell you what else is in that issue.

The contents page. This page is near the front of the magazine. It lists all the articles and tells you what page they appear on.

Before you read a magazine article, look at its structure. The article may include the following features.

The title. Articles' titles are sometimes worded cleverly. This helps get the reader's attention.

Pictures. Drawings or photographs usually appear along with an article. **Captions** tell what the pictures show.

Sidebars. Many articles have shorter articles set off from the main text. They tell more about the topic.

Into the Article

Mars is not a very human-friendly planet. Nevertheless, NASA plans to send people to Mars before the year 2020. This article explains what some astronauts are doing to prepare for the journey.

1 **S**o far only robots have gone to Mars. Sending robots costs less than sending humans. Scientists have thought that humans going to Mars would need enough oxygen and water for three years. Their rocket would need enough fuel
5 to get them home. Oxygen and rocket fuel take up a lot of room and cost a lot of money.

   Scientists are studying new ways to live on Mars. Astronauts could live in inflatable houses. Oxygen and rocket fuel can be made on Mars. Air and water can be re-used.

10 In 1997, engineer John Lewis took part in a test to see if four people could live in a place where everything was used over and over. Nothing was to be wasted.

   For three months Lewis and the others were shut up inside a three-story room. They washed their hands in

The Earthlings are coming! The Earthlings are coming!

Engineers at the National Aeronautics and Space Administration (NASA), in Houston, Texas, are preparing to send people to Mars. The mission is not official yet. "But it will happen," says John Connolly, NASA mission designer. "Probably before 2020."

Scientists give many reasons for going: to explore, to learn new things, to find important minerals, and maybe eventually to establish colonies so people can live there. But perhaps the most exciting reason to go is to search for evidence of past or present life, probably microscopic, on Mars.

"I want to believe it's there," says Connolly. "But the surface of Mars is a pretty nasty place. We may have to dig down to where we think it's wetter and warmer."

The mission will require an extended stay on a frozen planet that lacks breathable oxygen and has only trace amounts of water on its surface. Keep reading to learn how NASA is planning to get humans there and then keep them alive and safe.

From "Destination: Mars" by Aline Alexander Newman adapted from *National Geographic World*, January 2000, pp. 14–18. Copyright © 2000 by **National Geographic Society.** Retold by Holt, Rinehart and Winston. Reproduced by permission of the publisher.

Here's HOW

TEXT STRUCTURE: MAGAZINES

I like the title of this article. The word *Destination* tells me that someone or something is planning to make a trip to Mars! I'll read on to find out more.

Here's HOW

TEXT STRUCTURE: MAGAZINES

I wonder *why* people want to go to Mars. The sidebar feature, "The Earthlings are coming!," answers this question. It says that scientists want to explore the planet, look for minerals, and maybe even set up colonies.

Your TURN

VOCABULARY

The word *inflatable* means "able to be filled with air or another gas." A balloon is inflatable. Re-read lines 7–9 and underline the words that describe how an inflatable house will be used on Mars.

Here's HOW

VOCABULARY

I'm pretty sure that the word *recycled* (line 15) means "used again." I know the prefix *re-* means to do again, and to *cycle* something is to send it around.

Your TURN

TEXT STRUCTURE

What does the photograph here show?

_____

_____

How do you know what it shows?

_____

_____

Your TURN

TEXT STRUCTURE: MAGAZINES

Read the sidebar "Comparing Earth and Mars." Then, write one new fact you have learned.

_____

_____

15 recycled sweat. They even drank each other's urine! Sounds disgusting, right? It wasn't. All the body wastes were brought together and made pure. "Our drinking water was cleaner than tap water," says Lewis.

"Our final goal," says aerospace engineer Scott Baird, "is
20 to live off the land." Before the astronauts arrive on Mars, a cargo carrier will drop off a large chemical maker and an inflatable house.

It will take six months for astronauts to go to Mars. They will make a close study of Mars for five hundred days. Their
25 landing craft, made larger by attaching inflatable rooms, will be their home.

"It'll be a blast," says Baird. "By the time the kids of today grow up, they may be able to go."

Inside the "can," the nickname for the simulated capsule, the crew lived as they would during a long space voyage. Cut off from the world, they kept busy by exercising, maintaining the life-support systems, and keeping written logs.

COMPARING EARTH AND MARS

Nickname: the Blue Planet
Length of day: 23 hours, 56 minutes
Length of year: 365 days
Moons: one
Planet surface: mostly wet and warm
Atmosphere: 98 percent oxygen and nitrogen mix
Weather highlights: temperatures range from below −100°F to above 120°F; most storms wet

Nickname: the Red Planet
Length of day: 24 hours, 37 minutes
Length of year: 687 Earth days
Moons: two
Planet surface: cold and dry
Atmosphere: 95 percent carbon dioxide
Weather highlights: almost always below freezing; dry dust storms

Parts of a Magazine

Magazines have special parts that help you know what's inside. These are the **cover** and the **contents page.** Study the illustration below. Then label the parts on the lines provided.

The Circuit

Literary Focus: Tone

Tone is a speaker's attitude. Tone can be serious or lighthearted, happy or sad, calm or angry. When you talk to people, you know how they feel about something by their tone of voice. When you read, though, you can't hear the narrator's voice. You have to find the words and details in the story that communicate tone.

Reading Skill: Making Inferences

Reading is a lot like being a detective. Writers don't always tell you directly what's happening or how a narrator feels. You need to **make inferences,** or educated guesses, about the story. To make inferences, put together the clues in the story and think about what you already know.

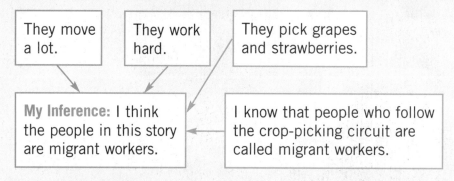

Into the Story

This story takes place in the 1950s. It follows a family as they travel along a "circuit," the path followed by migrant workers from harvest to harvest. The family is originally from Mexico. Why do you think this family came to the United States? What kind of difficulties do you think they will face? Think about how the lives of immigrants may have changed since the 1950s. What has stayed the same?

THE CIRCUIT

BASED ON THE STORY BY
Francisco Jiménez

1 It was that time of year again. The peak of the strawberry season was over.

As we drove home, Papá did not say a word. With both hands on the wheel, he stared at the dirt road. My older

5 brother, Roberto, was also silent. He leaned his head back and closed his eyes. Once in awhile he cleared from his throat the dust that blew in from outside.

Yes, it was that time of the year. When I opened the front door to the shack, I stopped. Everything we owned was

10 neatly packed in cardboard boxes. Suddenly, I felt even more the weight of hours, days, weeks, and months of work. I sat down on a box. The thought of having to move to Fresno brought tears to my eyes.

That night I could not sleep. I lay in bed thinking about

15 how much I hated this move.

A little before five o'clock in the morning, Papá woke everyone up. My little brothers and sisters screamed and yelled. To them, it was a great adventure. While we packed the breakfast dishes, Papá went outside to start the car.

20 Papá parked the car in front and left the motor running. "Listo,"[1] he yelled. Without saying a word, Roberto and I began to carry the boxes out to the car.

As we drove away, I felt a lump in my throat. I turned around and looked at our shack for the last time.

25 At sunset we drove into a labor camp near Fresno. Since Papá did not speak English, Mama asked the camp foreman[2] if he needed any more workers. "We don't need no more," said

---

1. **listo** (LEES toh): Spanish for "ready."
2. **foreman:** the person in charge; supervisor.

"The Circuit" by **Francisco Jiménez** adapted from *Cuentos Chicanos: A Short Story Anthology,* edited by Rodolfo A. Anaya and Antonio Marquez. Copyright © 1984 by the University of New Mexico Press. Published for *New America* by the University of New Mexico Press. Retold by Holt, Rinehart and Winston. Reproduced by permission of the author.

the foreman. "Check with Sullivan down the road. Can't miss him. He lives in a big white house with a fence around it."

30 We got work at Mr. Sullivan's for the whole season. He told us we could stay in an old garage near the stables.[3] The garage was worn out by the years. It had no windows.

That night we unpacked and cleaned our new home. Roberto swept away the loose dirt. Papá plugged the holes in
35 the walls with old newspapers. Mama fed my little brothers and sisters.

Early next morning, Mr. Sullivan showed us where his crop was. After breakfast, Papá, Roberto, and I headed for the vineyard to pick.

40 Around nine o'clock the temperature had risen to almost one hundred degrees. I was completely soaked in sweat. I picked up a jug of water and began drinking. "Don't drink too much. You'll get sick," Roberto shouted. But I already felt sick to my stomach. I dropped to my knees. My eyes were
45 glued on the hot sandy ground. Slowly I began to recover. I poured water over my face and neck.

I still felt a little dizzy when we took a break to eat lunch. We ate underneath a large tree that was on the side of the road. Suddenly, I noticed Papá's face turn pale. He was
50 looking down the road. "Here comes the school bus," he whispered loudly. Roberto and I ran and hid in the vineyards. We did not want to get in trouble for not going to school.

After lunch we went back to work. The sun kept beating down. The afternoon seemed to last forever. Finally, it was
55 too dark to continue picking.

Papá signaled to us that it was time to quit work. When we arrived home, we took a cold shower underneath a water

---

3. **stables** (STAY buhlz): building where horses and other animals stay.

Here's HOW

MAKING INFERENCES

Mr. Sullivan lives in a big white house. The narrator's family lives in an old garage near where the animals live. I bet the narrator's family is upset by the difference in living situations. On second thought, though, the family moves so much. Maybe they're used to living in shacks. I guess they don't expect to live like the Sullivans.

Your TURN

MAKING INFERENCES

Why is Papá alarmed when he sees the school bus?

_____

_____

_____

_____

_____

_____

_____

_____

Re-read lines 64–72. Underline the sentence that explains why the narrator is excited.

How does the narrator feel by the end of the paragraph? Why have his feelings changed?

_____

_____

_____

_____

_____

Mark with a slash (/) the part in the passage where the tone changes. Now, read the passage aloud. Use the appropriate tones of voice to mark the change.

Here's
HOW

MAKING
INFERENCES

I can tell from lines 85-92 that the narrator is very nervous about his first day at school. I think the narrator feels a lot of pressure to do well. He doesn't want to keep working in the fields.

hose. We then sat down to eat dinner. Some wooden crates[4] served as our table.

60   The next morning I could hardly move. My body ached all over. I felt little control over my arms and legs. This feeling went on every morning for days. Eventually my muscles got used to the work, though.

It was Monday, the first week of November. The grape
65 season was over. I could now go to school. I woke up early that morning. I was excited to start sixth grade. I decided to get up and join Papá and Roberto at breakfast. I sat at the table across from Roberto, but I kept my head down. I did not want to look up and face him. I knew he was sad. He
70 was not going to school today. He was not going tomorrow, or next week, or next month. He wasn't going until the cotton season was over. That was sometime in February.

When Papá and Roberto left for work, I felt relief. Two hours later, around eight o'clock, I stood by the side of the
75 road waiting for school bus number twenty. When it arrived, I climbed in. I sat in an empty seat in the back.

The bus stopped in front of the school. I felt very nervous. I walked to the principal's office. When I entered, I heard a woman's voice say: "May I help you?" I was startled. I hadn't
80 heard English for months. I struggled for English words. Finally, I managed to tell her that I wanted to enroll in sixth grade. After answering many questions, I was led to the classroom.

Mr. Lema, the sixth-grade teacher, greeted me and
85 assigned me a desk. He then introduced me to the class. I was so nervous and scared. Mr. Lema walked up to me and handed me an English book. He asked me to read. "We are on page 125," he said politely. I felt my blood rush to my

---

4. crates (krayts): boxes for packing.

head. I felt dizzy. "Would you like to read?" he asked. I
90 opened the book to page 125. My mouth was dry. My eyes
began to water. I could not begin. "You can read later,"
Mr. Lema said understandingly.

For the rest of the period I kept getting angrier and angrier
with myself. *I should have read,* I thought to myself.

95 During recess I went into the restroom. I opened my
English book to page 125. I began to read in a low voice. I
pretended I was in class. There were many words I did not
know. I closed the book and headed back to the classroom.

Mr. Lema was sitting at his desk correcting papers. When
100 I entered, he looked up at me and smiled. I felt better. I
walked up to him and asked if he could help me with the
new words. "Gladly," he said.

The rest of the month I spent my lunch hours working on
English with Mr. Lema, my best friend at school. One Friday,
105 Mr. Lema even offered to teach me how to play the trumpet.

That day I could hardly wait to get home to tell Papá and
Mama the great news. As I got off the bus, my little brothers
and sisters ran up to meet me. They were yelling and
screaming. I thought they were happy to see me. But then I
120 opened the door to our shack. I saw that everything we
owned was neatly packed in cardboard boxes.

Your
TURN
TONE

What does the narrator think
of Mr. Lema?

_____

_____

Underline the words
and phrases that reveal
the narrator's tone
(lines 91–105).

Your
TURN
TONE

Re-read the last paragraph.
1. What is the narrator's
tone at the beginning of this
paragraph?

_____

_____

2. Why does the narrator's
tone change when he
notices the packed
cardboard boxes? What do
the boxes mean?

_____

_____

_____

_____

_____

Making Inferences About Tone

Narrators don't always say directly "I feel depressed about this" or "I feel so happy." As a reader, you sometimes need to **make inferences,** or educated guesses, about what a narrator feels about something. When you talk to people, you can tell how they feel by their tone of voice. To figure out a **narrator's tone,** you need to look for clues in the story and think about what you already know.

"Thought Bubbles" Frames

Creating thought bubbles can help you make inferences about what a narrator is feeling. Fill out a thought bubble for each of the following moments from "The Circuit." In the bubbles, write the thoughts that explain the narrator's feelings. One of the thought bubbles has been filled in for you.

The family leave their shack to go on the road to look for work. (lines 1–24)

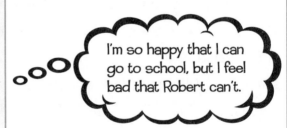

I'm so happy that I can go to school, but I feel bad that Robert can't.

The narrator finds out he's going to start school. (lines 64–72)

The narrator stays after class to get extra help from Mr. Lema. (lines 99–105)

When the narrator returns home, he sees packed cardboard boxes. (lines 119–121)

Vocabulary

Match each word in the **word bank** at right with its correct definition below. Write the matching word on the blank in front of the correct definition. Then, use the word in a sentence of your own. Write your sentence on the blank lines after the definition. Number 4 has been done for you.

Word Bank
circuit (title)
shack (line 24)
foreman (line 26)
stables (line 31)
crates (line 58)

1. _____ building where horses and other animals stay.

_____

_____

2. _____ person in charge; supervisor.

_____

_____

3. _____ boxes for packing.

_____

_____

4. circuit _____ regular route of a person doing a certain job.

The mail carrier makes the same circuit every day.

_____

5. _____ small, often temporary, living place; hut.

_____

Cesar Chavez: He Made a Difference

Reading Skill: Cause and Effect

A **cause** is the reason something happens. An **effect** is the result of a cause. Say you drop a glass of milk. The cause of this event would be that you let go of the glass. An effect of the event would be spilled milk. Another effect might be broken glass. You could show the cause and one of its effects like this:

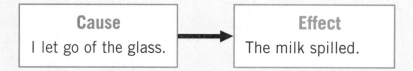

Cause	Effect
I let go of the glass.	The milk spilled.

Writers sometimes use a cause-and-effect pattern in their writing. One cause leads to an effect, which causes another effect, and so on. As you read this article, look for a major cause and some of the effects that follow it.

Into the Article

Many years ago, farm workers in California had poor working and living conditions. They were paid very little. They had no education. One of those workers, Cesar Chavez, set out to change these conditions. In 1962, Chavez formed a union. A union is a group whose purpose is to get fair pay and better working conditions for its members. It took years of difficult struggles, but the farm workers finally succeeded— against the odds.

Based on the Article by
Flo Ota De Lange

Cesar Chavez:
He Made a Difference

1   **S**ome people see unfairness and do nothing. Others fight unfairness to themselves and other people. Cesar Chavez (1927–1993) was someone who fought unfairness.

    The Chavez family were migrant farm workers in
5 California. They moved from farm to farm, picking crops[1] in the hot sun for low wages.[2] Cesar Chavez went to school only when the harvests[3] were finished. He had to quit school after eighth grade.

    One year Chavez's father saw the chance to own his
10 own land. He agreed to clean up eighty acres[4] of land and receive another forty acres as payment for his work. In the end, Chavez's father was cheated out of the forty acres.

    Cesar Chavez never forgot this injustice. All his life he had seen people like his father work hard in the fields but remain
15 poor. Chavez hoped to change this.

    In 1962, Chavez organized a union[5]—the United Farm Workers of America—to get fair wages and better working conditions for the farmerworkers. The union went on strike[6] against California's grape growers. Many people across the
20 United States refused to buy or eat grapes until the strike was settled.

    The union's actions were based on nonviolent principles. By practicing nonviolence himself, Chavez inspired others to struggle for justice through nonviolence.

25   When Cesar Chavez died in 1993, more than fifty thousand people gathered to honor him at the union's field office in Delano, California. The field office is called Forty Acres.

---

1. **crops** (krahps): plants grown or gathered by people for food or some other use.
2. **wages** (WAY jihz): money paid for work.
3. **harvests** (HAHR vihsts): times when food is gathered from fields.
4. **acres** (AY kuhrz): a measure of land, 43,560 square feet.
5. **union** (YOON yuhn): a group of workers joined together to protect their interests.
6. **strike** (stryk): a stopping of normal activities as a form of protest, usually so that an employer meets workers' demands.

Cause and Effect

A **cause** is the reason something happens. An **effect** is what happens as a result of the cause.

Cause   ⟶   Effect

Cause-and-Effect Chart

The causes and effects below come from "Cesar Chavez: He Made a Difference." For each cause, write an effect. For each effect, write a cause. Some have been done for you.

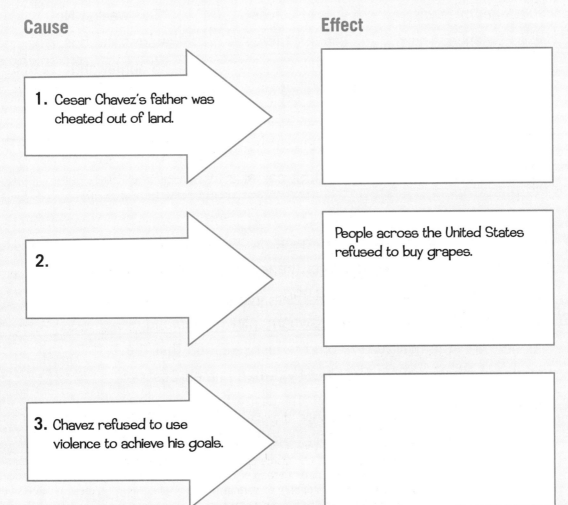

Cause

Effect

1. Cesar Chavez's father was cheated out of land.

2.

    People across the United States refused to buy grapes.

3. Chavez refused to use violence to achieve his goals.

Picking Strawberries: Could You Do It?

Reading Skill: Drawing Conclusions

A **conclusion** is your final thought about something you have read. You can draw a conclusion about an entire article or about a paragraph or section within an article.

Before you draw a conclusion, first look at the facts in the article. The facts in the article should lead you to your conclusion.

Fact: Lance opened his eyes and glanced lazily at the clock.	**Fact:** A slow smile spread across Lance's face.	**Fact:** He thought "Two weeks! No alarms, no bus, no homework!"

Conclusion:

Lance is enjoying the first day of a two-week vacation.

Into the Article

Strawberry picking may be one of the lowest-paying farm jobs in the country. In the late 1990s, a group called the United Farm Workers helped strawberry pickers demand higher pay. (You may recall from the last selection that the United Farm Workers was started by a man named Cesar Chavez.)

Picking Strawberries:
Could You Do It?

Based on the Article by
Flo Ota De Lange

Here's
HOW

DRAWING CONCLUSIONS

After reading the first paragraph, I think that a strawberry picker doesn't make much money. The facts lead me to this conclusion. For example, a worker must pick 10,000 strawberries a day. Also, a worker must work a twelve-hour day to make enough money to support his or her family.

Your
TURN

DRAWING CONCLUSIONS

Re-read the entire article. What conclusion can you draw about picking strawberries?

Now underline three facts that lead you to your conclusion.

1 The following experiment[1] will give you an idea of what it is like to pick strawberries for a living. One problem with picking a strawberry is that a ripe berry is easily bruised. If it is bruised, no one will buy it. So the strawberry picker
5 must pick the berry off the plant without hurting it. Sound easy? Well, maybe so—if you have all the time in the world and are picking only one berry. But what if you have to earn enough money to provide for your family? Then, you have to pick about ten thousand strawberries in a twelve-hour
10 workday. That turns strawberry picking into a very different job, doesn't it?

To pick ten thousand strawberries in twelve hours, you have to pick about

• 1 strawberry every four seconds
15 • 14 strawberries every minute
• 840 strawberries every hour

So how can we get an idea of what the strawberry picker's hands are doing as she or he picks a berry? Let's use a twelve-inch length of string in place of a strawberry plant.
20 Tie this piece of string around something firm, like a chair back or a door handle. Then, tie a granny knot[2] in the string. Have someone keep track of how long it takes for you to do it. How fast can you tie the knot? Practice doing it until you can tie a granny knot in four seconds or less. Then, try doing
25 the same thing with fourteen separate lengths of twelve-inch string. The idea is to get fourteen separate knots tied in less than a minute. Now, imagine tying 840 knots in an hour and 10,080 knots in twelve hours. Are you getting an idea of what strawberry picking is like?

---

1. **experiment** (ehk SPEHR uh mehnt): a test to find out something.
2. **granny knot** (naht): a loose knot, like a square knot but with the ends crossed the wrong way.

Drawing Conclusions

A **conclusion** is your final thought about something you have read. Before you draw a conclusion about an article, first look at the facts. The facts should lead you to your conclusion.

Find three facts in the article you just read. Write them in the boxes below. Now think: What conclusion can you draw from these facts? Write your conclusion in the box at the bottom of the page. One of the facts has been filled in for you.

Fact:	Fact:	Fact: Picking strawberries to make a living is like tying 10,080 knots in twelve hours.

Conclusion:

The Diary of Anne Frank, Act One, Scenes 1 and 2

Literary Focus: Theme

Theme is what a story has to tell us about life. It's the message that we take away from the story. You can figure out a theme from the words and ideas in the story. In particular, look at

title: Does the author hint at a theme in the title?

characters: How do the characters change?

big moments: What do the most dramatic moments seem to say about life?

Remember that the meaning of the story comes from both the author and the reader. Because each reader is different, readers come up with different themes.

Reading Skill: Making Inferences

An **inference** is an educated guess. You make inferences when you put together what you see and hear in the play with what you already know. In a play, you can make inferences not only from the words the characters say, but also from their actions and from the setting.

Into the Play

This is a true story—Anne Frank was a real person. The Frank family and four other Jews hid for more than two years in a few small rooms above Mr. Frank's office and warehouse. In August 1944, the Nazi police raided their hiding place and sent them to concentration camps. Of the eight people who went into hiding, only Mr. Frank survived.

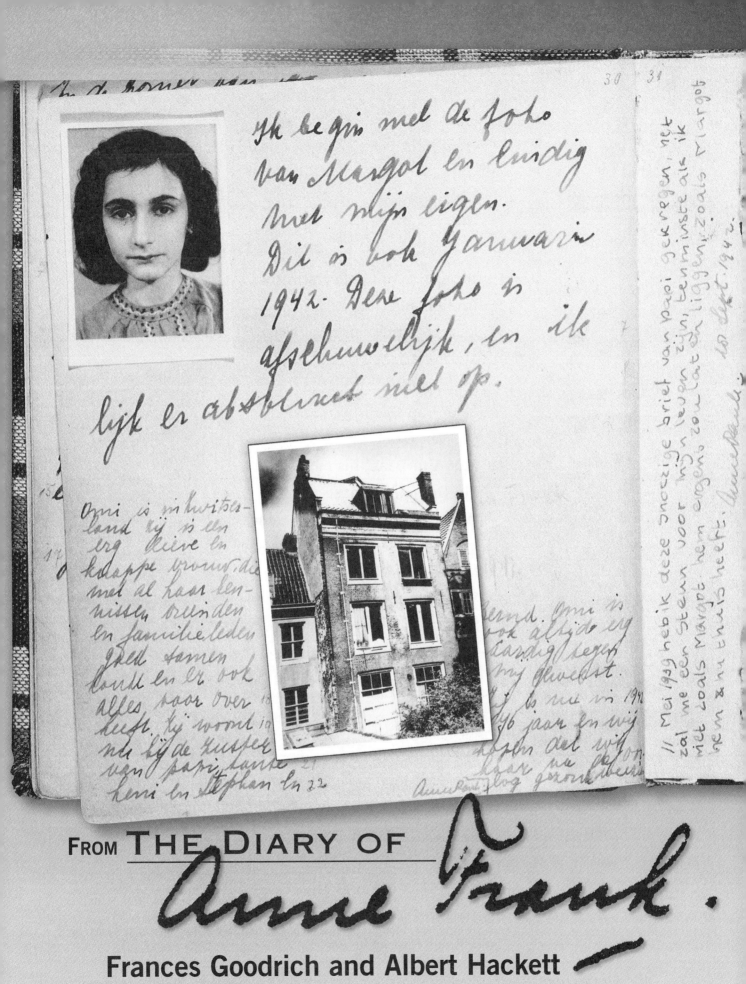

FROM THE DIARY OF Anne Frank.

Frances Goodrich and Albert Hackett

Your
TURN

VOCABULARY

What do you think is the meaning of the word *annex* in the heading "Occupants of the Secret Annex"? Read lines 1–4 before you write your answer.

_____

_____

_____

Here's
HOW

THEME

The title of the play is <u>The Diary of Anne Frank</u>. I wonder if there's a clue about a theme in there. I think of a diary as a journal about everyday events—normal stuff. But living in hiding must have been far from normal. Anne's diary must be very unlike other girls' diaries.

YOU NEED TO KNOW *The Diary of Anne Frank* takes place in the Dutch city of Amsterdam. Before you read the play, note the list of characters and the setting. Most of the play is told in the form of a flashback—a break in the action going on in the present that shows events that happened in the past.

Characters

Occupants of the Secret Annex:

Anne Frank

Margot Frank, her older sister

Mr. Frank, their father

Mrs. Frank, their mother

Peter Van Daan

Mr. Van Daan, his father

Mrs. Van Daan, his mother

Mr. Dussel, a dentist

Workers in Mr. Frank's Business:

Miep Gies,[1] a young Dutchwoman

Mr. Kraler,[2] a Dutchman

Setting: Amsterdam, the Netherlands, July 1942 to August 1944; November 1945. Netherlands and Holland are the same country. The people and language of the Netherlands are called Dutch.

Act One

• SCENE 1

1   *The scene remains the same throughout the play. It is the top floor of a warehouse and office building in Amsterdam,*

---

1. **Miep Gies** (meep khees).
2. **Kraler** (KRAH luhr).

From *The Diary of Anne Frank* (play) by Albert Hackett and Frances Goodrich. Copyright © 1956 by Albert Hackett, Frances Goodrich Hackett, and Otto Frank; copyright renewed © 1986 by Albert Hackett, David Huntoon, and Frances Neuwirth. Reproduced by permission of **Random House, Inc.** Electronic format by permission of **Flora Roberts, Inc.**

Holland. The sharply peaked roof of the building is outlined
5 *against a sea of other rooftops stretching away into the*
distance. Nearby is the belfry[3] of a church tower, the
Westertoren, whose carillon[4] rings out the hours.
Occasionally faint sounds float up from below: the voices of
children playing in the street, the tramp of marching feet, a
10 *boat whistle from the canal.[5]*

The three rooms of the top floor and a small attic space
above are exposed to our view. The largest of the rooms is
in the center, with two small rooms, slightly raised, on either
side. On the right is a bathroom, out of sight. A narrow,
15 *steep flight of stairs at the back leads up to the attic. The*
rooms are sparsely furnished, with a few chairs, cots, a table
or two. The windows are painted over or covered with
makeshift blackout curtains.[6] In the main room there is a
sink, a gas ring for cooking, and a wood-burning stove for
20 *warmth.*

The room on the left is hardly more than a closet. There
is a skylight[7] in the sloping ceiling. Directly under this room
is a small, steep stairwell, with steps leading down to a
door. This is the only entrance from the building below.
25 *When the door is opened, we see that it has been*
concealed on the outer side by a bookcase attached to it.

The curtain rises on an empty stage. It is late afternoon,
November 1945.

The rooms are dusty, the curtains in rags. Chairs and
30 *tables are overturned.*

The door at the foot of the small stairwell swings open.

MR. FRANK *comes up the steps into view. He is a gentle,*

Your
TURN

VOCABULARY

What do you think is the meaning of the word *sparsely* as it appears in line 16? Underline the words in lines 16–17 that help you figure out this meaning.

_____

_____

Here's
HOW

MAKING INFERENCES

When I read lines 29–30, I can infer that no one has been in the room for a while. Facts that help me make this inference are the dusty room, the ragged curtains, and the overturned furniture. No one has taken care of things in the room for a long time.

---

3. belfry (BEHL free): bell tower.
4. carillon (KAR uh LAHN): set of bells, each of which produces a single tone.
5. canal: artificial waterway. Amsterdam, which was built on soggy ground, has
   more than one hundred canals, built to help drain the land. The canals are used
   like streets.
6. blackout curtains: curtains that cover the window at night so that no light
   shows outside.
7. skylight: window.

THE DIARY OF ANNE FRANK, ACT ONE, SCENES 1 AND 2 **69**

cultured[8] European in his middle years. There is still a trace of a German accent in his speech.

35   He stands looking slowly around, making a supreme effort at self-control. He is weak, ill. His clothes are threadbare.

    After a second he drops his rucksack on the couch and moves slowly about. He opens the door to one of the
40 smaller rooms and then abruptly closes it again, turning away. He goes to the window at the back, looking off at the Westertoren as its carillon strikes the hour of six; then he moves restlessly on.

    From the street below we hear the sound of a barrel
45 organ[9] and children's voices at play. There is a many-colored scarf hanging from a nail. MR. FRANK *takes it, putting it around his neck. As he starts back for his rucksack, his eye is caught by something lying on the floor. It is a woman's white glove. He holds it in his hand and*
50 *suddenly all of his self-control is gone. He breaks down crying.*

    We hear footsteps on the stairs. MIEP GIES *comes up, looking for Mr. Frank.* MIEP *is a Dutchwoman of about twenty-two. She wears a coat and hat, ready to go home.*
55 *She is pregnant. Her attitude toward* MR. FRANK *is protective, compassionate.[10]*

Miep. Are you all right, Mr. Frank?

Mr. Frank (*quickly controlling himself*). Yes, Miep, yes.

Miep. Everyone in the office has gone home. . . . It's after
60 six. (*Then, pleading*)[11] Don't stay up here, Mr. Frank. What's the use of torturing yourself like this?

---

8. **cultured** (KUHL chuhrd): civilized; well mannered; learned.
9. **barrel organ**: musical street instrument shaped like a barrel and played by winding a handle.
10. **compassionate** (kuhm PASH uhn iht): kind.
11. **pleading** (PLEE dihng): begging.

Mr. Frank. I've come to say goodbye . . . I'm leaving here, Miep.

Miep. What do you mean? Where are you going? Where?

65 **Mr. Frank.** I don't know yet. I haven't decided.

Miep. Mr. Frank, you can't leave here! This is your home! Amsterdam is your home. Your business is here, waiting for you. . . . You're needed here. . . . Now that the war is over, there are things that . . .

70 **Mr. Frank.** I can't stay in Amsterdam, Miep. It has too many memories for me. Everywhere, there's something . . . the house we lived in . . . the school . . . that street organ playing out there . . . I'm not the person you used to know, Miep. I'm a bitter[12] old man. *(Breaking off)* Forgive me. I

75 shouldn't speak to you like this . . . after all that you did for us . . . the suffering. . . .

Miep. No. No. It wasn't suffering. You can't say we suffered. *(As she speaks, she straightens a chair which is overturned.)*

80 **Mr. Frank.** I know what you went through, you and Mr. Kraler. I'll remember it as long as I live. *(He gives one last look around.)* Come, Miep. *(He starts for the steps, then remembers his rucksack, going back to get it.)*

Miep *(hurrying up to a cupboard)*. Mr. Frank, did you

85 see? There are some of your papers here. *(She brings a bundle of papers to him.)* We found them in a heap of rubbish on the floor after . . . after you left.

Mr. Frank. Burn them. *(He opens his rucksack to put the glove in it.)*

90 **Miep.** But, Mr. Frank, there are letters, notes . . .

Mr. Frank. Burn them. All of them.

Miep. Burn *this*? *(She hands him a paperbound notebook.)*

---

12. **bitter:** unaccepting.

MAKING INFERENCES

I can infer from lines 70–76 that Mr. Frank must have gone through something terrible to be so bitter and unhappy now.

MAKING INFERENCES

Re-read lines 84–89. What can you infer about Mr. Frank's feelings toward the bundle of papers?

_____

_____

_____

IN OTHER WORDS   Mr. Frank tells Miep that he
is leaving Amsterdam. He thanks her for what she and
Mr. Kraler did for them while they were in hiding.
Miep brings him a pile of his papers, and he says to
burn them. He does not want to remember the past.

Mr. Frank *(quietly).* Anne's diary. *(He opens the diary*
95 *and begins to read.)* "Monday, the sixth of July, nineteen
forty-two." *(To* MIEP*)* Nineteen forty-two. Is it possible,
Miep? . . . Only three years ago. *(As he continues his*
reading, he sits down on the couch.) "Dear Diary, since you
and I are going to be great friends, I will start by telling you
100 about myself. My name is Anne Frank. I am thirteen years
old. I was born in Germany the twelfth of June, nineteen
twenty-nine. As my family is Jewish, we emigrated to
Holland when Hitler came to power."

[*As* MR. FRANK *reads on, another voice joins his, as if*
105 *coming from the air. It is* ANNE'S *voice.*]

Mr. Frank and Anne's Voice. "My father started a
business, importing[13] spice and herbs. Things went well for
us until nineteen forty. Then the war came, and the Dutch
capitulation, followed by the arrival of the Germans. Then
110 things got very bad for the Jews."

[MR. FRANK*'s voice dies out.* ANNE*'s voice continues alone.*
The lights dim slowly to darkness. The curtain falls on
the scene.]

Anne's Voice. You could not do this and you could not do
115 that. They forced Father out of his business. We had to wear
yellow stars.[14] I had to turn in my bike. I couldn't go to a
Dutch school anymore. I couldn't go to the movies or ride in
an automobile or even on a streetcar, and a million other

---

13. **importing:** bringing into the country.
14. **yellow stars:** The Nazis ordered all Jews to sew a large Star of David (a six-
    pointed star) on their outer clothing so that they could be easily recognized
    as Jews.

things. But somehow we children still managed to have fun.

120 Yesterday Father told me we were going into hiding. Where, he wouldn't say. At five o'clock this morning Mother woke me and told me to hurry and get dressed. I was to put on as many clothes as I could. It would look too suspicious if we walked along carrying suitcases. It wasn't until we were on

125 our way that I learned where we were going. Our hiding place was to be upstairs in the building where Father used to have his business. Three other people were coming in with us . . . the Van Daans and their son Peter . . . Father knew the Van Daans but we had never met them. . . .

130   [*During the last lines the curtain rises on the scene. The lights dim on.* ANNE'*s voice fades out.*]

IN OTHER WORDS   Among the papers is Anne's diary. Mr. Frank begins to read from the diary. Anne is writing in 1942, and she is thirteen. She describes life under Nazi rule. All Jews have to wear a large yellow star sewn on their outer clothing. This is so they will be easily recognized as Jews. Jews are not allowed to live a normal life. They cannot go to school, ride bicycles, see movies, or do many other things. Now, Anne's family is going into hiding with another family, the Van Daans.

• **SCENE 2**

It is early morning, July 1942. The rooms are bare, as before, but they are now clean and orderly.

135   MR. VAN DAAN, *a tall, portly man in his late forties, is in the main room, pacing up and down, nervously smoking a cigarette. His clothes and overcoat are expensive and well cut.*[15]

---

15. **well cut**: well made.

THEME

In lines 114–119, Anne describes many of the restrictions that Nazis put on Jews in Holland starting in 1940. What does she say about how she and other children reacted? Underline the words.

Combine what you know about children with Anne's words. What general statement can you make about children's ability to deal with hardship?

_____

_____

_____

What do you think helped Anne cope?

_____

_____

Here's
HOW

VOCABULARY

I didn't know the meaning of the word *portly* in line 135 and there were no other words around *portly* to help me with the meaning. I looked up *portly* in a dictionary. It means "heavy of body." I think this is another way of saying Mr. Van Daan is fat.

   THE DIARY OF ANNE FRANK, ACT ONE, SCENES 1 AND 2   **73**

MRS. VAN DAAN *sits on the couch, clutching her possessions:*
140 *a hatbox, bags, etc. She is a pretty woman in her early forties. She wears a fur coat over her other clothes.*

PETER VAN DAAN *is standing at the window of the room on the right, looking down at the street below. He is a shy, awkward boy of sixteen. He wears a cap, a raincoat, and*
145 *long Dutch trousers, like plus fours.*[16] *At his feet is a black case, a carrier for his cat.*

The yellow Star of David is conspicuous on all of their clothes.

Mrs. Van Daan *(rising, nervous, excited).* Something's
150 happened to them! I know it!

Mr. Van Daan. Now, Kerli!

Mrs. Van Daan. Mr. Frank said they'd be here at seven o'clock. He said . . .

Mr. Van Daan. They have two miles to walk. You can't
155 expect . . .

Mrs. Van Daan. They've been picked up. That's what's happened. They've been taken . . .

[MR. VAN DAN *indicates*[17] *that he hears someone coming.*]

Mr. Van Daan. You see?

160 [PETER *takes up his carrier and his school bag, etc., and goes into the main room as* MR. FRANK *comes up the stairwell from below.* MR. FRANK *looks much younger now. His movements are brisk, his manner confident. He wears an overcoat and carries his hat and a small cardboard box. He*
165 *crosses to the* VAN DAANS, *shaking hands with each of them.*]

Mr. Frank. Mrs. Van Daan, Mr. Van Daan, Peter. *(Then, in explanation of their lateness)* There were too many of the Green Police[18] on the streets . . . we had to take the long way around.

---

16. **plus fours:** baggy trousers that end in cuffs just below the knee.
17. **indicates** (IHN duh KAYTS): shows.
18. **Green Police**: Nazi police, who wore green uniforms.

IN OTHER WORDS   It is July 1942. Mr. and Mrs. Van Daan wait in the hiding place with their teenage son, Peter. Mrs. Van Daan is very nervous. She is afraid the Franks have been caught by the Nazis. Then, Mr. Frank enters. He looks younger and healthier than in Scene 1.

170   [*Up the steps come* MARGOT FRANK, MRS. FRANK, MIEP (*not pregnant now*), *and* MR. KRALER. *All of them carry bags, packages, and so forth. The Star of David is conspicuous on all of the* FRANKS' *clothing.* MARGOT *is eighteen, beautiful, quiet, shy.* MRS. FRANK *is a young mother, gently bred,*[19]

175 *reserved. She, like* MR. FRANK, *has a slight German accent.* MR. KRALER *is a Dutchman, dependable, kindly.*

As MR. KRALER *and* MIEP *go upstage to put down their parcels,* MRS. FRANK *turns back to call* ANNE.]

Mrs. Frank. Anne?

180   [ANNE *comes running up the stairs. She is thirteen, quick in her movements, interested in everything, mercurial in her emotions. She wears a cape and long wool socks and carries a school bag.*]

Mr. Frank (*introducing them*). My wife, Edith. Mr. and

185 Mrs. Van Daan (MRS. FRANK *hurries over, shaking hands with them.*) . . . their son, Peter . . . my daughters, Margot and Anne.

[ANNE *gives a polite little curtsy as she shakes* MR. VAN DAAN'S *hand. Then she immediately starts off on a tour of*

190 *investigation of her new home, going upstairs to the attic room.*

IN OTHER WORDS   The others arrive: Mrs. Frank, Margot (Anne's older sister), Miep, and Mr. Kraler.

---

19. gently bred: well brought up; refined.

Your TURN

MAKING INFERENCES

The word *leisure* in line 196 means "free time." What inference can you make about Mr. Frank's personality from lines 195–196?

_____

_____

_____

Your TURN

VOCABULARY

The word *stores* in line 197 can mean "supplies for the future" or "places where goods are kept." Draw a line under the meaning it has here.

Anne comes last. Mr. Frank introduces his family to the Van Daans. Anne goes off to explore the hiding place that Miep and Mr. Kraler have set up for them.

MIEP *and* MR. KRALER *are putting the various things they have brought on the shelves.*]

Mr. Kraler. I'm sorry there is still so much confusion.

195 **Mr. Frank.** Please. Don't think of it. After all, we'll have plenty of leisure to arrange everything ourselves.

Miep (*to* MRS. FRANK). We put the stores of food you sent in here. Your drugs are here . . . soap, linen[20] here.

Mrs. Frank. Thank you, Miep.

200 **Miep.** I made up the beds . . . the way Mr. Frank and Mr. Kraler said. (*She starts out.*) Forgive me. I have to hurry. I've got to go to the other side of town to get some ration books[21] for you.

Mrs. Van Daan. Ration books? If they see our names on 205 ration books, they'll know we're here.

Mr. Kraler. There isn't anything . . .

Miep. Don't worry. Your names won't be on them. (*As she hurries out*) I'll be up later.

Mr. Frank. Thank you, Miep.

210 **Mrs. Frank** (*to* MR. KRALER). It's illegal, then, the ration books? We've never done anything illegal.

Mr. Frank. We won't be living here exactly according to regulations.

[*As* MR. KRALER *reassures* MRS. FRANK, *he takes various small* 215 *things, such as matches and soap, from his pockets, handing them to her.*]

---

20. **linen:** sheets, towels, pillowcases, and so forth.
21. **ration books:** books of stamps or coupons issued by the government during wartime. People could purchase scarce items such as food, clothing, and gasoline only with these coupons.

Mr. Kraler. This isn't the black market,[22] Mrs. Frank. This is what we call the white market . . . helping all of the hundreds and hundreds who are hiding out in Amsterdam.

220 [*The carillon is heard playing the quarter-hour before eight.* MR. KRALER *looks at his watch.* ANNE *stops at the window as she comes down the stairs.*]

Anne. It's the Westertoren!

Mr. Kraler. I must go. I must be out of here and 225 downstairs in the office before the workmen get here. *(He starts for the stairs leading out.)* Miep or I, or both of us, will be up each day to bring you food and news and find out what your needs are. Tomorrow I'll get you a better bolt for the door at the foot of the stairs. It needs a bolt that you 230 can throw yourself and open only at our signal. *(To* MR. FRANK*)* Oh . . . You'll tell them about the noise?

Mr. Frank. I'll tell them.

Mr. Kraler. Goodbye, then, for the moment. I'll come up again, after the workmen leave.

235 **Mr. Frank.** Goodbye, Mr. Kraler.

Mrs. Frank *(shaking his hand)*. How can we thank you?

[*The others murmur their goodbyes.*]

Mr. Kraler. I never thought I'd live to see the day when a man like Mr. Frank would have to go into hiding. When you 240 think—

IN OTHER WORDS Miep goes off to get the ration books that will allow her to buy food for the people in the Secret Annex. Mr. Kraler reveals that many Jews are in hiding in Amsterdam. Miep and Mr. Kraler are breaking the law by helping them. Mrs. Frank does not like doing anything illegal. But, under the Nazis, the law is no longer just.

---

22. **black market**: place or system for buying and selling goods illegally, without ration stamps.

Your TURN

MAKING INFERENCES

To protect the people hiding in the Secret Annex, Mr. Kraler says he is going to install a bolt on the door. Will this be enough protection? What can you infer is probably going to happen later?

_____

_____

_____

Here's HOW

MAKING INFERENCES

From what Mr. Kraler says in lines 238-240, I think he has a lot of respect for Mr. Frank. Maybe Mr. Frank was an important man.

Here's HOW

THEME

Mr. Kraler and Miep are risking a lot to take care of the Franks and the Van Daans. I wonder if I would be brave enough to help people in the Franks' situation.

VOCABULARY

The word *interval* can mean "the space between" or "time between." Draw a line under the meaning *interval* has in line 242.

VOCABULARY

What do you think the word *garment* means in line 248? Circle the words in lines 248–252 that help you figure out the meaning.

Your TURN

THEME

The meaning of "going into hiding" is starting to become clear. Life is not going to be normal. Underline the rules in lines 262–271 that you would find hard to follow. Then, explain whether you think the Franks and Van Daans will succeed in following these rules.

[*He breaks off, going out.* MR. FRANK *follows him down the steps, bolting the door after him. In the interval before he returns,* PETER *goes over to* MARGOT, *shaking hands with her. As* MR. FRANK *comes back up the steps,* MRS. FRANK

245 *questions him anxiously.*]

Mrs. Frank. What did he mean, about the noise?

Mr. Frank. First let us take off some of these clothes.

[*They all start to take off garment after garment. On each of their coats, sweaters, blouses, suits, dresses is another*

250 *yellow Star of David.* MR. *and* MRS. FRANK *are underdressed quite simply. The others wear several things: sweaters, extra dresses, bathrobes, aprons, nightgowns, etc.*]

Mr. Van Daan. It's a wonder we weren't arrested, walking along the streets . . . Petronella with a fur coat in July . . .

255 and that cat of Peter's crying all the way.

Anne (*as she is removing a pair of panties*). A cat?

Mrs. Frank (*shocked*). Anne, please!

Anne. It's all right. I've got on three more.

[*She pulls off two more. Finally, as they have all removed*

260 *their surplus*[23] *clothes, they look to* MR. FRANK, *waiting for him to speak.*]

Mr. Frank. Now. About the noise. While the men are in the building below, we must have complete quiet. Every sound can be heard down there, not only in the workrooms but in the

265 offices too. The men come at about eight-thirty and leave at about five-thirty. So, to be perfectly safe, from eight in the morning until six in the evening we must move only when it is necessary, and then in stockinged feet. We must not speak above a whisper. We must not run any water. We cannot use

270 the sink or even, forgive me, the w.c.[24] The pipes go down through the workrooms. It would be heard. No trash . . .

(MR. FRANK *stops abruptly as he hears the sound of*

---

23. **surplus**: extra.
24. **w.c.**: short for "water closet," or toilet.

marching feet from the street below. Everyone is motionless, paralyzed with fear. MR. FRANK *goes quietly into the room on*
275 *the right to look down out of the window.* ANNE *runs after him, peering out with him. The tramping feet pass without stopping. The tension*[25] *is relieved.* MR. FRANK, *followed by* ANNE, *returns to the main room and resumes his instructions to the group.*) . . . No trash must ever be thrown out which
280 might reveal that someone is living up here . . . not even a potato paring. We must burn everything in the stove at night. This is the way we must live until it is over, if we are to survive.

[*There is silence for a second.*]

285 **Mrs. Frank.** Until it is over.

Mr. Frank (*reassuringly*)[26]. After six we can move about . . . we can talk and laugh and have our supper and read and play games . . . just as we would at home. (*He looks at his watch.*) And now I think it would be wise if we
290 all went to our rooms, and were settled before eight o'clock. Mrs. Van Daan, you and your husband will be upstairs. I regret that there's no place up there for Peter. But he will be here, near us. This will be our common room, where we'll meet to talk and eat and read, like one family.

IN OTHER WORDS   Mr. Kraler leaves. The others begin to undress. Because they could not be seen with suitcases, they are wearing as many clothes as they could put on. It is July, so they are very hot. Mr. Frank tells them that they must be silent all day when there are workers in the building.

295 **Mr. Van Daan.** And where do you and Mrs. Frank sleep?

Mr. Frank. This room is also our bedroom.

---

25. **tension** (TEHN shuhn): strain.
26. **reassuringly** (REE uh SHOOR ihng lee): in a way that restores confidence.

Here's HOW

VOCABULARY

I wasn't sure about the meaning of *paralyzed* (line 274). But when I looked at the word that comes right before it—*motionless*—I knew that *paralyzed* means "not moving." The people were too afraid to move.

Your TURN

VOCABULARY

What is a potato "paring," mentioned in line 281? To make a "paring," you would have to "pare" something. What do you think *pare* means?

_____

_____

_____

Mrs. Van Daan. That isn't right. We'll sleep here and you take the room upstairs.

Mr. Van Daan. It's your place.

300 **Mr. Frank.** Please. I've thought this out for weeks. It's the best arrangement. The only arrangement.

Mrs. Van Daan (*to* MR. FRANK). Never, never can we thank you. (*Then, to* MRS. FRANK) I don't know what would have happened to us, if it hadn't been for Mr. Frank.

305 **Mr. Frank.** You don't know how your husband helped me when I came to this country . . . knowing no one . . . not able to speak the language. I can never repay him for that. (*Going to* MR. VAN DAAN) May I help you with your things?

Mr. Van Daan. No. No. (*To* MRS. VAN DAAN) Come along,
310 liefje.[27]

Mrs. Van Daan. You'll be all right, Peter? You're not afraid?

Peter (*embarrassed*). Please, Mother.

[*They start up the stairs to the attic room above.* MR. FRANK
315 *turns to* MRS. FRANK.]

Mr. Frank. You too must have some rest, Edith. You didn't close your eyes last night. Nor you, Margot.

Anne. I slept, Father. Wasn't that funny? I knew it was the last night in my own bed, and yet I slept soundly.

320 **Mr. Frank.** I'm glad, Anne. Now you'll be able to help me straighten things in here. (*To* MRS. FRANK *and* MARGOT) Come with me. . . . You and Margot rest in this room for the time being. (*He picks up their clothes, starting for the room on the right.*)

325 **Mrs. Frank.** You're sure . . . ? I could help . . . And Anne hasn't had her milk . . .

Mr. Frank. I'll give it to her. (*To* ANNE *and* PETER) Anne, Peter . . . it's best that you take off your shoes now, before

---

27. **liefje** (LEEF yah): Dutch for "little dear one."

Your
TURN

VOCABULARY

Does the phrase "you didn't close your eyes" in lines 316–317 mean that Mrs. Frank really did not close her eyes all night? Explain your answer.

_____

_____

_____

_____

_____

_____

you forget. *(He leads the way to the room, followed by*
330 MARGOT.*)*

Mrs. Frank. You're sure you're not tired, Anne?

Anne. I feel fine. I'm going to help Father.

Mrs. Frank. Peter, I'm glad you are to be with us.

Peter. Yes, Mrs. Frank.

335 [MRS. FRANK *goes to join* MR. FRANK *and* MARGOT.

During the following scene MR. FRANK *helps* MARGOT *and*
MRS. FRANK *to hang up their clothes. Then he persuades them*
both to lie down and rest. The VAN DAANS, *in their room*
above, settle themselves. In the main room ANNE *and* PETER
340 *remove their shoes.* PETER *takes his cat out of the carrier.*]

IN OTHER WORDS Mr. and Mrs. Van Daan go
upstairs to unpack. Mr. Frank tells his wife and Margot
that they should rest. He and Anne will arrange things.
Unlike her mother and sister, Anne is cheerful and does
not seem worried. Peter takes his cat out of its carrier.

Anne. What's your cat's name?

Peter. Mouschi.[28]

Anne. Mouschi! Mouschi! Mouschi! *(She picks up the cat,*
walking away with it. To PETER*)* I love cats. I have one . . . a
345 darling little cat. But they made me leave her behind. I left
some food and a note for the neighbors to take care of
her. . . . I'm going to miss her terribly. What is yours? A
him or a her?

Peter. He's a tom.[29] He doesn't like strangers. *(He takes*
350 *the cat from her, putting it back in its carrier.)*

Anne *(unabashed).* Then I'll have to stop being a
stranger, won't I? Is he fixed?

Peter *(startled).* Huh?

---

28. **Mouschi:** (MOO shee).
29. **tom:** male cat.

THE DIARY OF ANNE FRANK, ACT ONE, SCENES 1 AND 2   **81**

Here's
HOW

THEME

Anne is so cheerful. I don't
know if it's because she is
new to this situation, she's
young, or that's just the
way she is. I would be so
depressed. I'm going to pay
attention to her moods to
see how they change the
longer she is in hiding.

Here's
HOW

VOCABULARY

I think the word *unabashed*
in line 351 means "not
embarrassed" because Anne
does not stop trying to get
Peter to talk to her. Because
the word is in parentheses,
it tells the actor how to say
that line.

Here's
HOW

VOCABULARY

A penknife (line 364) is not a knife made out of a pen; it is a pocketknife. I don't know why it's called a penknife; it doesn't make sense to me. Maybe I will look up the history of this word later.

Your
TURN

VOCABULARY

What does Peter mean when he says he is "a lone wolf" in line 367?

_____

_____

_____

Anne. Did you have him fixed?

355   **Peter.** No.

Anne. Oh, you ought to have him fixed—to keep him from—you know, fighting. Where did you go to school?

Peter. Jewish Secondary.

Anne. But that's where Margot and I go! I never saw you
360 around.

Peter. I used to see you . . . sometimes . . .

Anne. You did?

Peter. . . . in the schoolyard. You were always in the middle of a bunch of kids. *(He takes a penknife from his*
365 *pocket.)*

Anne. Why didn't you ever come over?

Peter. I'm sort of a lone wolf. *(He starts to rip off his Star of David.)*

Anne. What are you doing?

370 **Peter.** Taking it off.

Anne. But you can't do that. They'll arrest you if you go out without your star.

[*He tosses his knife on the table.*]

Peter. Who's going out?

IN OTHER WORDS Anne is eager to make friends with Peter and his cat, Mouschi. But Peter does not seem very friendly. They find that they went to the same school, although they never met each other. To Anne's shock, Peter begins ripping the star off his shirt. She says he will be arrested. He points out that they will not be going outside anymore.

375 **Anne.** Why, of course! You're right! Of course we don't need them anymore. *(She picks up his knife and starts to take her star off.)* I wonder what our friends will think

when we don't show up today?

Peter. I didn't have any dates with anyone.

380 **Anne.** Oh, I did. I had a date with Jopie to go and play ping-pong at her house. Do you know Jopie de Waal?[30]

Peter. No.

Anne. Jopie's my best friend. I wonder what she'll think when she telephones and there's no answer? . . . Probably

385 she'll go over to the house. . . . I wonder what she'll think . . . we left everything as if we'd suddenly been called away . . . breakfast dishes in the sink . . . beds not made . . . *(As she pulls off her star, the cloth underneath shows clearly the color and form of the star.)* Look! It's still there! *(PETER goes over to*

390 *the stove with his star.)* What're you going to do with yours?

Peter. Burn it.

Anne. *(She starts to throw hers in, and cannot.)* It's funny, I can't throw mine away. I don't know why.

Peter. You can't throw . . . ? Something they branded you

395 with . . . ? That they made you wear so they could spit on you?

Anne. I know. I know. But after all, it is the Star of David, isn't it?

[*In the bedroom, right,* MARGOT *and* MRS. FRANK *are lying*

400 *down.* MR. FRANK *starts quietly out.*]

Peter. Maybe it's different for a girl.

[MR. FRANK *comes into the main room.*]

Mr. Frank. Forgive me, Peter. Now let me see. We must find a bed for your cat. *(He goes to a cupboard.)* I'm glad

405 you brought your cat. Anne was feeling so badly about hers. *(Getting a used small washtub)* Here we are. Will it be comfortable in that?

Peter *(gathering up his things).* Thanks.

---

30. **Jopie de Waal:** (YOH pee duh VAHL).

Your TURN

THEME

Re-read lines 389–398. Underline what Peter does with his Star of David patch. Circle what Anne does with hers. Then, summarize what the patch has meant (or what you think it has meant) to each of them:
To Peter it means

_____

_____

To Anne it means

_____

_____

Here's HOW

VOCABULARY

I wanted to know what the Star of David (line 397) looked like. I looked in a dictionary, and it said that this star has six points. It is made up of two interlaced triangles. The Star of David is a symbol of Judaism, the religion of the Jews and of Israel.

Your
TURN

MAKING
INFERENCES

Re-read lines 409–418.
Then, draw a line under the
words that show that Mr.
Frank was trying to make
Peter feel more comfortable
and happy.

Here's
HOW

MAKING
INFERENCES

In lines 424–425, Anne
seems to be upset about
the months she will have to
spend in the Secret Annex.
In line 427, Mr. Frank points
to a box that he wants Anne
to open. I think he is trying to
cheer Anne up. For Anne, or
for me, too, having to live for
months in the same room
would be awful.

Mr. Frank *(opening the door of the room on the left).* And

410 here is your room. But I warn you, Peter, you can't grow
anymore. Not an inch, or you'll have to sleep with your feet
out of the skylight. Are you hungry?

Peter. No.

Mr. Frank. We have some bread and butter.

415 **Peter.** No, thank you.

Mr. Frank. You can have it for luncheon then. And
tonight we will have a real supper . . . our first supper
together.

Peter. Thanks. Thanks. *(He goes into his room. During the*

420 *following scene he arranges his possessions in his new room.)*

IN OTHER WORDS Anne wonders what their
friends will think when they find out the families have
disappeared. She takes her star off, too. Peter is
burning his, but Anne cannot. To her, the Star of
David is still a Jewish symbol, not just a Nazi
punishment. Mr. Frank welcomes the cat and shows
Peter to his room.

Mr. Frank. That's a nice boy, Peter.

Anne. He's awfully shy, isn't he?

Mr. Frank. You'll like him, I know.

Anne. I certainly hope so, since he's the only boy I'm

425 likely to see for months and months.

[MR. FRANK *sits down, taking off his shoes.*]

Mr. Frank. Annele,[31] there's a box there. Will you open

it? [*He indicates a carton on the couch.* ANNE *brings it to the*

center table. In the street below, there is the sound of

430 *children playing.*]

---

31. Annele (AHN uh luh): Yiddish for "little Anne" (like "Annie").

Anne *(as she opens the carton).* You know the way I'm going to think of it here? I'm going to think of it as a boardinghouse.[32] A very peculiar summer boardinghouse, like the one that we— *(She breaks off as she pulls out some*
435 *photographs.)* Father! My movie stars! I was wondering where they were! I was looking for them this morning . . . and Queen Wilhelmina![33] How wonderful!

Mr. Frank. There's something more. Go on. Look further.

(He goes over to the sink, pouring a glass of milk from a
440 *thermos bottle.)*

Anne *(pulling out a pasteboard-bound book).* A diary! *(She throws her arms around her father.)* I've never had a diary. And I've always longed for one. *(She looks around the room.)* Pencil, pencil, pencil, pencil. *(She starts down the*
445 *stairs.)* I'm going down to the office to get a pencil.

> **IN OTHER WORDS** Anne and her father talk about Peter and his shyness. Mr. Frank has a box for Anne. It has her treasured photos of movie stars and the queen. It also has a new diary. Anne is thrilled. She wants to run down to the office for a pencil.

Mr. Frank. Anne! No! *(He goes after her, catching her by the arm and pulling her back.)*

Anne *(startled).* But there's no one in the building now.

Mr. Frank. It doesn't matter. I don't want you ever to go
450 beyond that door.

Anne *(sobered).*[34] Never . . . ? Not even at nighttime, when everyone is gone? Or on Sundays? Can't I go down to listen to the radio?

---

32. **boardinghouse**: a place that takes paying guests.
33. **Queen Wilhelmina** (WIHL hehl MEE nah) (1880–1962): queen of the Netherlands from 1890 to 1948.
34. **sobered**: made serious.

Your TURN

MAKING INFERENCES

Re-read lines 441–445. What can you infer about Anne's future use of the diary that her father has given her?

_____

_____

_____

Mr. Frank. Never. I am sorry, Anneke.[35] It isn't safe. No,
455 you must never go beyond that door.

[*For the first time* ANNE *realizes what "going into hiding" means.*]

Anne. I see.

Mr. Frank. It'll be hard, I know. But always remember this,
460 Anneke. There are no walls, there are no bolts, no locks that anyone can put on your mind. Miep will bring us books. We will read history, poetry, mythology. (*He gives her the glass of milk.*) Here's your milk. (*With his arm about her, they go over to the couch, sitting down side by side.*) As a matter of fact,
465 between us, Anne, being here has certain advantages for you. For instance, you remember the battle you had with your mother the other day on the subject of overshoes?[36] You said you'd rather die than wear overshoes? But in the end you had to wear them? Well now, you see, for as long as we are here,
470 you will never have to wear overshoes! Isn't that good? And the coat that you inherited from Margot, you won't have to wear that anymore. And the piano! You won't have to practice on the piano. I tell you, this is going to be a fine life for you!

IN OTHER WORDS Mr. Frank stops her. He explains that she must never leave their hiding place, even when there is no one in the building. Anne is shocked. She begins to realize what being in hiding really means. Mr. Frank tries to cheer her up. She can read; she won't have to wear overshoes; she won't have to practice the piano.

475 [ANNE'S *panic is gone.* PETER *appears in the doorway of his room, with a saucer in his hand. He is carrying his cat.*]

---

35. **Anneke** (AHN uh kuh): another affectionate nickname for Anne.
36. **overshoes**: waterproof shoe covers.

Peter. I . . . I . . . I thought I'd better get some water for Mouschi before . . .

Mr. Frank. Of course.

480 [*As he starts toward the sink, the carillon begins to chime[37] the hour of eight. He tiptoes to the window at the back and looks down at the street below. He turns to* PETER, *indicating in pantomime[38] that it is too late.* PETER *starts back for his room. He steps on a creaking board. The three of*
485 *them are frozen for a minute in fear. As* PETER *starts away again,* ANNE *tiptoes over to him and pours some of the milk from her glass into the saucer for the cat.* PETER *squats on the floor, putting the milk before the cat.* MR. FRANK *gives* ANNE *his fountain pen and then goes into the room at the right.*
490 *For a second* ANNE *watches the cat; then she goes over to the center table and opens her diary.*

In the room at the right, MRS. FRANK *has sat up quickly at the sound of the carillon.* MR. FRANK *comes in and sits down beside her on the settee,[39] his arm comfortingly around her.*
495 *Upstairs, in the attic room,* MR. *and* MRS. VAN DAAN *have hung their clothes in the closet and are now seated on the iron bed.* MRS. VAN DAAN *leans back, exhausted.* MR. VAN DAAN *fans her with a newspaper.*

ANNE *starts to write in her diary. The lights dim out; the*
500 *curtain falls.*

In the darkness ANNE'S *voice comes to us again, faintly at first and then with growing strength.*]

Anne's Voice. I expect I should be describing what it feels like to go into hiding. But I really don't know yet myself.
505 I only know it's funny never to be able to go outdoors . . . never to breathe fresh air . . . never to run and shout and

---

37: **chime**: ring.
38. **indicating in pantomime** (PAN tuh MYM): acting out rather than speaking.
39. **settee**: small couch.

Your
TURN

THEME

Earlier you thought about whether anyone could live by the rules at the annex (lines 262–271). Read the stage directions in lines 480–499 and Anne's diary entry in lines 503–509. Think about whether you could live as you see the Franks and Van Daans living and as Anne describes here in her diary. Then, explain what you think enables people to live in this way.

jump. It's the silence in the nights that frightens me most. Every time I hear a creak in the house or a step on the street outside, I'm sure they're coming for us. The days aren't so
510 bad. At least we know that Miep and Mr. Kraler are down there below us in the office. Our protectors, we call them. I asked Father what would happen to them if the Nazis found out they were hiding us. Pim[40] said that they would suffer the same fate that we would. . . . Imagine! They know this,
515 and yet when they come up here, they're always cheerful and gay, as if there were nothing in the world to bother them. . . . Friday, the twenty-first of August, nineteen forty-two. Today I'm going to tell you our general news. Mother is unbearable. She insists on treating me like a baby, which I loathe.[41]
520 Otherwise things are going better. The weather is . . .

[As ANNE's _voice is fading out, the curtain rises on the scene._]

IN OTHER WORDS   Peter wants to turn on the sink to give his cat water. But it's too late; the clock outside chimes eight. The workers would hear him. Anne gives the cat some of her milk. Mr. Frank gives Anne a pen and she begins to write in her diary. As the scene closes, she reads aloud from her diary. She describes what it is like to be in hiding: the boredom, the lack of fresh air, the fear of being caught.

---

40. Pim: family nickname for Mr. Frank.
41. loathe (loh_th_): hate.

Identifying a Theme

Theme is a story's message about life. Thinking about the two scenes you read from *The Diary of Anne Frank,* see if you can identify a theme. Look back at the Here's How examples and at your responses to the Your Turn activities about theme. Then, answer questions in the chart below. Some sample responses have been provided for you.

Title What clues about theme might the title reveal?	I'm not sure if there is a clue about theme in the title. If there is, it might be something about the idea of a diary and how a diary is usually about everyday things, and the play is about everyday people trying to live their everyday lives under really awful conditions.
Characters How do the characters change? What do they discover about life?	_____ _____ _____ _____ _____
Big Moments Which scenes were the most dramatic? What did they say to you about life?	One dramatic moment was the time when Anne took off her Star of David patch. Anne couldn't burn the patch because the Star of David itself was still a positive symbol to her. _____ _____ _____
One theme of *The Diary of Anne Frank* is _____. I say this because _____.	

Camp Harmony *and* In Response to Executive Order 9066

Literary Focus: Recurring Themes

Who am I? How should I live my life? People over the ages have had basically the same dreams, fears, and questions about life. That's why the same themes come up again and again—or recur—in the stories people tell. These common themes are called **recurring themes.** For example, *Good can triumph over evil* can be found in ancient texts as well as in contemporary novels.

Reading Skill: Making Generalizations

A **generalization** is a statement based on several smaller examples. When you make a generalization, you look at separate pieces of information. Then you make a broad statement about them. For example, during a trip to the grocery store you might make this generalization.

 This apple is large.

That apple is very small.

Here are more small apples.

 Most of the apples in this store are small.

Into the Autobiography and the Poem

Imagine that your family has been told that you all must leave your home tomorrow. The government has decided that you are a threat to your country. Besides a bag for bedding and two suitcases for clothes, you can take only your school backpack. What would you choose to take in your backpack?

Camp Harmony

Based on the Autobiography by
Monica Sone

In Response to Executive Order 9066

Dwight Okita

Background

Many thousands of Japanese Americans were sent to internment camps in 1942. The United States had gone to war with Japan. The government feared that the Japanese Americans would not be loyal to the United States. Executive Order 9066 was a government order that made it legal to lock up these people. Most of the 120,000 Japanese Americans spent three years behind barbed wire. They were let out in 1945, at the end of World War II. They returned home to find their property stolen. Other people had taken their jobs. The Japanese Americans had to wait more than forty years for the U.S. government to apologize and give them money to make up for their losses.

Lines 8–16 give lots of details about the family's room. It was small, empty, and had a bare floor with weeds growing through it. If I put all of these small details together, I can make this generalization: *The family's living conditions were very poor.*

Here's
HOW

In line 16, what does the word *cultivate* mean? I reread the sentences about the dandelions to look for clues. Mother is happy to see the dandelions and wants them to stay there. Maybe she wants to grow them. *Cultivate* must mean "to raise plants."

Here's
HOW

Dandelions are just weeds! Why does Mrs. Sone want to grow more of them? Well, Mrs. Sone is a very positive person. She tries to make the best of bad situations. Some people are always able to see the good.

Camp Harmony

1 Our bus turned a corner and drove through a gate into what looked like a chicken farm. The guard stepped out of the bus and stood beside the door. The young man who had put us into the buses called out, "OK, folks, all off at
5 Yokohama,[1] Puyallup."[2]

We had arrived at the internment[3] camp called Camp Harmony.

Our family would be living in one room at the end of a low barracks[4] about two blocks long. Our one room was the
10 size of a living room. There was one small window in the wall opposite the door. The room was bare except for a small, wood-burning stove crouching in the center. The floor was made by laying two-by-fours[5] on the ground. Dandelions were growing up through the cracks; Mother was delighted
15 when she saw them. "Don't anyone pick the dandelions. I'm going to cultivate them."

Father snorted, "Grow more of them? If we don't watch out, those things will be growing out of our hair."

Mother said, "They're the only beautiful things around
20 here. We could have a garden right in here."

My brother Henry said, "Are you joking, Mama?"

I said, "She has to have some inspiration[6] to write poems."

---

1. **Yokohama** (YOH kuh HAH muh): second-largest port city in Japan.
2. **Puyallup** (pyoo A luhp): small town in the state of Washington. When the bus driver says, "Yokohama, Puyallup," he's trying to make a joke. He's saying that Puyallup is about to become a Japanese city.
3. **internment** (ihn TURN muhnt): confinement; being locked away.
4. **barracks** (BAR uhks): buildings usually used to house soldiers.
5. **two-by-fours:** boards that are two inches thick and four inches across.
6. **inspiration** (IHN spuh RAY shuhn): source for creative ideas.

Mother and Father went out to see what the other folks
25 were doing. Mother returned shortly, her face lit up with a
smile, "We're in luck. The toilet is right nearby, so we won't
have to walk far."

We laughed at our wonderful mother who could be both
poetic and practical. Father came back, loaded down with
30 stacks of boards over his shoulder, his pockets full of nails.
Father dumped the boards in a corner and said, "There was a
pile of wood left by the carpenters and hundreds of nails
scattered loose. Now we can have tables and chairs."

At lunchtime we went to the mess hall[7] where we found a
35 long line of people. Lunch was two canned sausages, one
piece of boiled potato, and a slice of bread. I had to force
myself to eat.

We cheered up when trucks delivered our cots.[8] Henry
arranged them. Father and Mother were in the corner nearest
40 the wood stove. In the other corner, Henry placed two cots
for my sister Sumi and me. His cot was in the corner nearest
the door.

We were glad we had a room at the end of the building,
because we had just one neighbor to worry about. The wall
45 separating the rooms was open at the top, so Mrs. Funai next
door could tell when Sumi was sitting up in bed in the dark,
putting her hair up. "Mah, Sumi-chan," Mrs. Funai would say
through the plank[9] wall, "are you curling your hair tonight,
again?" Sumi would glare angrily at the wall.

50 We had to be inside our room by nine o'clock every
night. Lights had to be out by ten. At night, all through
the barracks, there was the sound of creaking cots, crying
babies, and coughing people. At first the fire in our little
wood stove was so hot that I was afraid it would melt right

Your TURN

MAKING GENERALIZATIONS

Re-read Sumi's experience with Mrs. Funai in lines 43–49. Then make a generalization about Sumi's reaction to living in the camp.

_____

_____

Here's HOW

RECURRING THEMES

Even in this horrible camp, Sumi curls her hair every night. I've seen this theme before when I read about Anne Frank: Even in the worst circumstances, people do ordinary things.

7. **mess hall:** building where a large number of people eat their meals.
8. **cots:** beds.
9. **plank:** a wooden board.

In lines 74–76, the author says that she is in the camp because she has Japanese ancestors. I think she is talking about her grandparents and their parents going back a long way. That is what *ancestors* are—relatives from long ago.

In lines 66–79, the author tries to answer the question "Who am I?" She shares her feelings about her identity. How does the author feel about being a Japanese American? How does she feel about being in the camp?

_____

_____

_____

_____

_____

_____

_____

_____

55 down to the floor. The fire lasted for only a short time, and then the cold made the room feel like a deep freeze. As it grew quieter in the barracks, I could hear the light patter of rain. Soon I felt the splat! splat! of raindrops on my face. I finally had to get out and move my cot to the center of the

60 room.

I stared at our little window, unable to sleep. A powerful beam of light moved across the window every few seconds. The lights came from the high towers that were all around the camp. Guards with submachine guns[10] kept watch over

65 us day and night.

I thought about the wire fence that was all around us and felt angry. Why was I being kept behind a fence, like a criminal? I was an American but I was not being treated like one. It seemed that my American citizenship wasn't real.

70 Then what was I? I was not a citizen of Japan, as my parents were. Father and Mother had little to do with Japan. They had lived twenty-five years in America and, like any other citizen, they had worked and paid their taxes.

Of one thing I was sure. The wire fence was real. I did

75 not have the right to walk out of it because I had Japanese ancestors. I could not be trusted to be loyal to the idea of democracy.[11] Camp Harmony would make sure I was loyal. I finally buried my face in my pillow to wipe out my angry thoughts and get what sleep I could.

---

10. **submachine guns:** machine guns.
11. **democracy:** the form of government in the United States of America.

In Response to Executive Order 9066:
All Americans of Japanese Descent Must Report to Relocation Centers

1 **D**ear Sirs:
Of course I'll come. I've packed my galoshes
and three packets of tomato seeds. Denise calls them
"love apples." My father says where we're going
5 they won't grow.

I am a fourteen-year-old girl with bad spelling
and a messy room. If it helps any, I will tell you
I have always felt funny using chopsticks
and my favorite food is hot dogs.
10 My best friend is a white girl named Denise—
we look at boys together. She sat in front of me
all through grade school because of our names:
O'Connor, Ozawa. I know the back of Denise's head very
   well,
I tell her she's going bald. She tells me I copy on tests.
15 We're best friends.

I saw Denise today in Geography class.
She was sitting on the other side of the room.
"You're trying to start a war," she said, "giving secrets
   away
to the Enemy. Why can't you keep your big mouth shut?"
20 I didn't know what to say.

"In Response to Executive Order 9066" from *Crossing with the Light* by Dwight
Okita. Copyright © 1992 by **Dwight Okita.** Published by Tia Chucha Press, Chicago.
Reproduced by permission of the author.

Here's HOW

VOCABULARY

What are *galoshes* (line 2)?
I looked in the dictionary
and found out that they are
overshoes you wear in the
snow. My grandmother told
me that her galoshes had
buckles.

Your TURN

MAKING GENERALIZATIONS

How old is the speaker?

_____

What's the speaker's favorite
food?

_____

What does she do with her
best friend?

_____

From these details, you can
make this generalization:
The speaker is

an ordinary kid/ the enemy
(Circle one.)

1. In lines 16–20, Denise accuses the speaker of "giving secrets away to the Enemy." How does that passage make you feel? Why?

_____

_____

_____

2. In lines 21–24, the speaker doesn't reply to Denise. Instead, she gives her tomato seeds. How does that passage make you feel?

_____

_____

_____

What do you think this poem says about how people should act toward each other?

_____

_____

_____

_____

I gave her a packet of tomato seeds
and asked her to plant them for me, told her
when the first tomato ripened
she'd miss me.

Recurring Themes

A **theme** is a story's message about life. Certain themes have been repeated again and again in literature throughout the ages. These themes are called **recurring themes.**

Below are some of the themes you can find in the two selections you have just read. On the first blank line for Theme 1 (a), tell how the theme is shown in one of the selections. On the second blank line (b), try to name another story, song, movie, or TV show where you recognize the same theme. Then, explain how it was shown there. Finally, try to think of a third recurring theme in the selections and complete the box. Theme 2 has been filled in for you.

Theme 1: When fear sweeps over a nation, certain groups suffer terrible injustices.

(a) _____

_____

(b) _____

_____

Theme 2: People do ordinary things even in extraordinary circumstances.

(a) In "Camp Harmony," Sumi curls her hair every night.

(b) In *The Diary of Anne Frank,* Peter and Anne do their homework, and Mr. and Mrs. Frank play chess.

Theme 3:

(a) _____

_____

(b) _____

_____

The Gettysburg Address

Literary Focus: Refrain

A **refrain** is a sound, word, phrase, line, or group of lines that is said again. A refrain creates an echo in the listener's ear. It builds rhythm and helps stress important points. As you read the Gettysburg Address, look for repeated sounds, words, and phrases. How do they strengthen Lincoln's message?

Reading Skill: Dialogue with the Text

When you enter into a **dialogue with the text,** you focus on what you don't understand, ask questions about those parts, and then try to answer the questions. Use a chart like this one.

Questions	Responses
Four score and seven years ago? How many years is that? What date is he talking about?	Score = 20 years 4 x 20 = 80; 80 + 7 = 87 years Lincoln's speech was given in 1863. 1863 minus 87 years = 1776. That's the year our nation was founded. (I never thought I'd have to do arithmetic in English class!)

Into the Speech

The Battle of Gettysburg took place in 1863, during the Civil War. In that bloody three-day battle, Union forces stopped Confederate forces from moving north. The battle left at least 51,000 soldiers dead, wounded, or missing. When the battlefield was dedicated as a cemetery, President Abraham Lincoln was asked to make a speech. His speech is thought to be one of the greatest speeches ever made by a United States leader.

Executive Mansion,

Washington, _____, 186_

Four score and seven years ago our fathers brought forth, upon this continent, a new nation, conceived in liberty, and dedicated to the proposition that "all men are created equal.

Now we are engaged in a great civil war, testing whether that nation, or any nation so conceived, and so dedicated, can long endure. We are met on a great battle field of that war. We have come to dedicate a portion of it, as a final resting place for those who died here, that that nation might live. This we may, in all propriety do. But, in a larger sense, we can not dedicate—we can not consecrate—we can not hallow, this ground—

The Gettysburg Address

Based on the Speech by
Abraham Lincoln

1   Four score and seven[1] years ago, our fathers formed a new nation on this continent.[2] This nation was founded on freedom, and it was dedicated[3] to the idea that all men are created equal.

5   Now we are engaged[4] in a great civil war. We are testing whether that nation, or any nation like it, can last. We meet here on a great battlefield of that war. We have come to dedicate part of that field to the people who died here so that their nation would live. It is proper that we should do this.

10   But, in a larger sense,[5] we cannot dedicate this ground or make it holy. Brave men, living and dead, struggled here. They have made this ground holy, not us. The world won't remember what we say here, but it will never forget what these brave men did here. The job of the living is to finish the

15   work that the brave men here fought for. We must dedicate ourselves to this great task.[6] We should feel increased devotion to the cause because these brave men died here. We must be determined that these men should not have died in vain.[7] We must make sure this nation, under God, will have

20   a new birth of freedom, and that government of the people, by the people, and for the people will not disappear from the earth.

---

1. **four score and seven:** eighty-seven.
2. **continent** (KAHN tuh nuhnt): land mass; in this case, North America.
3. **dedicated** (DEHD uh KAY tihd): set apart for a special purpose.
4. **engaged** (ehn GAYJD): involved.
5. **sense:** meaning.
6. **task:** a job; duty that needs to be done.
7. **in vain:** without success; uselessly.

Refrain Chart

A **refrain** is a sound, word, phrase, line, or group of lines that is said again. Speakers use refrains to please the listener's ear and to stress important points. In the left-hand side of the chart below are line numbers from "The Gettysburg Address." Re-read each set of lines. Then, in the right-hand side of the chart, list repeated sounds, words, or phrases. One has been done for you.

Quotations from the Speech	Repeated Sounds, Words, or Phrases
Lines 1–4	
Lines 5–9	The word *we* is repeated five times. Three of those times it appears at the beginning of a sentence.
Lines 15–19 [Hint: Look carefully at the beginnings of the sentences in these lines.]	
Lines 19–22	

from I Have a Dream

Literary Focus: Allusion

Have you ever quoted a line from a favorite movie? If so, you have alluded to that movie. An **allusion** is a reference to something that most people know about. Martin Luther King, Jr., adds power and beauty to his words by using allusions.

Reading Skill: Noting Style

Style is the way a speaker or a writer uses language. One writer might use simple words and sentences. Another might use poetic language, repeated words, or strong rhythms. Use these sentence starters to take notes about King's unique use of language.

King likes to use words such as . . .

King likes to repeat phrases such as . . .

Into the Speech

Have you ever dreamt about the future? What would you like to see? What are your hopes and dreams for the future? In this speech, Martin Luther King, Jr., tells what his dream is for the future of all Americans.

from *I Have a Dream*

Based on the Speech by
Martin Luther King, Jr.

Background

On August 28, 1963, more than 200,000 Americans took part in a march in Washington, D.C. The people wanted Congress to pass a civil rights bill. This bill would give equal rights to African Americans. People from all races and from almost every state were in the march. All day, they gathered in front of the Lincoln Memorial to sing songs and listen to speeches.

The day was almost over when Dr. Martin Luther King, Jr., began to speak. He started out by describing how African Americans were denied all the rights and benefits that America gives its other citizens. Then, he put aside the speech he had written and began to speak from his heart. He shared his dream of America. This dream was heard across the country. It touched the hearts of his listeners. King's words still have the power to touch our hearts today.

1   My friends, I have a dream.

I have a dream that one day this nation will live out the true meaning of its creed:[1] " . . . that all men are created equal."

I have a dream that one day the sons of former slaves and
5 the sons of former slaveowners will sit down together at the table of brotherhood.

I have a dream that my children will one day live in a nation where they will not be judged by the color of their skin but by the content of their character.

10 I return with this dream to the South. There we will work and pray together, fight together, stand up for freedom together, knowing that we will be free one day.

One day all children will sing, "My country 'tis of thee, sweet land of liberty, of thee I sing. Land where my fathers
15 died, land of the pilgrim's pride, from every mountainside, let freedom ring."

If America is to be a great nation, this must become true. So let freedom ring from the hilltops of New Hampshire and from the mountains of New York. Let freedom ring from the
20 Alleghenies[2] of Pennsylvania, the snowcapped Rockies of Colorado, the peaks of California!

But not only that; let freedom ring from Stone Mountain of Georgia, from Lookout Mountain of Tennessee, and from every hill in Mississippi.

25 When freedom rings everywhere, that is the day when all people—black and white, Jews and Gentiles,[3] Protestants and Catholics—will join hands and sing, "Free at last! Thank God almighty, we are free at last!"

---

1. **creed:** statement of beliefs or principles.
2. **Alleghenies** (A luh GAY neez): Allegheny Mountains.
3. **Gentiles** (JEHN tylz): people who are not Jews, especially Christians.

Adapted from "I Have a Dream" by Martin Luther King, Jr. Copyright © 1963 by Martin Luther King, Jr.; copyright renewed © 1991 by Coretta Scott King. Retold by Holt, Rinehart and Winston. Reproduced by permission of **The Estate of Martin Luther King, Jr., c/o Writers House as agent for the proprietor.**

Allusion

Allusions are references to things that most people already know. A writer or speaker may allude to history, religion, sports, music, or other people's words. In the left-hand column are some allusions from "I Have a Dream." In the right-hand column, tell where these allusions come from. Re-read Dr. King's speech and the notes in the side margin. Then, see if you can fill in the empty spaces. One has been done for you.

Allusion in "I Have a Dream"	Where the Allusion Comes From
1. "all men are created equal"	**1.**
2. "My country 'tis of thee . . . let freedom ring."	**2.** The song "America," also known as "My Country 'Tis of Thee."
3. "Free at last! Thank God almighty, we are free at last."	**3.**

from The Power of Nonviolence

Reading Skill: Taking Notes and Outlining

Have you ever wanted to tell a friend about an exciting article you just read—but had trouble remembering the best parts? **Taking notes** and **making an outline** can help you keep track of an article's main ideas and details.

1. Make Notes on Note Cards

Another Main Idea:

Main Idea:
Details that support this idea.
1. Detail
2. Detail

3. Outline

Title of the Article

  I. First main idea

    A. Supporting detail

    B. Supporting detail

    C. Supporting detail

  II. Second main idea

2. Use Notes to Write Outline

Into the Article

This article tells one person's experience during the civil rights movement of the 1950s and 1960s. Up to that time, some parts of our nation were segregated. Black people could not be with white people in public places. They could not eat at the same restaurants, go to the same schools, or use the same water fountains. During the 1960s, people began demanding that African Americans be given the same rights as white people. Read on to learn how some people made these demands—and how other people responded.

Based on the Oral History by
John Lewis

from # The
Power *of*
Nonviolence

YOU NEED TO KNOW   Nonviolence is the practice of not using violence to gain what you want. Nonviolence has a long history.

Two thousand years ago, Jesus gave a nonviolent response to injustice—"But I tell you, do not resist an evil person. If someone strikes you on the right cheek, turn to him the other also." That's where we get our expression "turn the other cheek."

In the 1800s, Henry David Thoreau used civil disobedience—a nonviolent breaking of the law—when he refused to pay his taxes. He did not believe in slavery. The U.S. government supported slavery with its citizens' taxes. Thoreau went to jail for his beliefs.

In the 1940s, Mohandas K. Gandhi led the people of India in their struggle for independence from Britain. Indians joined in nonviolent refusals to attend government schools and pay taxes. Eventually, India gained independence from Great Britain. This long history gives strength to nonviolent protests such as the one described by John Lewis.

1   When I was a boy in the little town of Troy, I saw signs saying "White" and "Colored"[1] on the water fountains. At the theater the white people sat downstairs, and we had to go upstairs.

5   In February 1960, five hundred college students, black and white, showed up for the first nonviolent lunch-counter sit-in.

Our list of "Rules of the Sit-in" said things like, "Sit up straight, don't talk back, don't hit back."

---

1. **colored:** dark skinned.

From "John Lewis: Hand in Hand Together" (retitled "The Power of Nonviolence") adapted from *From Camelot to Kent State* by Joan Morrison and Robert K. Morrison. Copyright © 1987 by Joan Morrison and Robert K. Morrison. Retold by Holt, Rinehart and Winston. Reproduced by permission of **Times Books, a division of Random House, Inc.** Electronic format by permission of *John A. Ware Literary Agency.*

Hundreds of well-dressed young people sat down at lunch
10 counters and waited to be served.

After we sat down, the lunch counter would be closed. Sometimes they would lock the door and turn out all the lights. We would continue to sit.

The police watched us being attacked. A mob of young
15 white men came in and pulled people off the lunch-counter stools. They crushed burning cigarettes out in our hair or faces, poured ketchup and hot sauce all over us, pushed us down to the floor, and beat us. The police came in and arrested over one hundred students. They charged us with
20 disorderly conduct,[2] and we were all sentenced to a fifty-dollar fine or thirty days in jail. We wouldn't pay the fine, so we were put in jail.

The protests continued when the students were released from jail. In April 1960, the lunch counters were
25 desegregated.

That was the power of nonviolence.

I think the nonviolent movement changed us, black and white alike. We are a different people, now. We are better people—a little more human.

Your TURN

TAKING NOTES

What is the main idea of the paragraph that begins with line 14?

_____

_____

_____

Here's HOW

TAKING NOTES

Some details I will list from the paragraph that begins on line 14 are
1. protesters pulled off lunch-counter stools
2. burning cigarettes put out in protesters' hair
3. protesters put in jail

Your TURN

VOCABULARY

What do you think the word *sentenced* means in line 20? Underline the words that help you figure out this meaning.

_____

_____

_____

---

2. **disorderly conduct:** unruly or bad behavior.

Writing an Outline

An **outline** shows the main ideas and important details of an article. Below is an outline of "The Power of Nonviolence." Some words have been left out of the outline. Re-read the article and complete the outline.

The Power of Nonviolence

I. John Lewis grew up in the segregated South.

   A. He grew up in a town called _____.

   B. Troy's water fountains were _____.

   C. Troy's _____ were also segregated.

II. Lewis took part in a lunch-counter _____ in 1960.

   A. Hundreds of young people sat down at lunch counters.

   B. The counters were _____.

   C. _____ were attacked and hurt.

   D. Many of the protesters were put in _____.

III. The sit-ins were successful.

   A. After the protesters were released, they _____.

   B. The lunch counters were in _____ April 1960.

   C. _____ made our society better.

Vocabulary

Prefixes

A **prefix** is a group of letters that comes at the beginning of a word. A prefix has a meaning all its own. When a prefix is attached to the front of another word, the new word has a new meaning. For example, *un* is a prefix that means "not" or "the opposite of." When *un* is put at the front of the word *safe*, the new word is unsafe, or "not safe." *Unsafe* is the opposite of *safe.*

In the left-hand column below are prefixes used in "The Power of Nonviolence." Draw a line from the prefix to the word it is attached to in the selection. Then, use the word in a sentence of your own. One has been done for you.

1. non   orderly

2. de   violence

3. dis   segregate

1. My sentence: _____

_____

2. My sentence: _____

_____

3. My sentence: _____

_____

The Tell-Tale Heart

Literary Focus: Narrator

A **narrator** is a person or a character who tells a story. Some narrators can be trusted. They report events logically and honestly. Other narrators, though, *cannot* be trusted. As you read "The Tell-Tale Heart," decide how you feel about its narrator. Can you trust him, or not?

Reading Skill: Previewing and Making Predictions

Part of the fun of reading is guessing what will happen next. When you do this, you are **making predictions.** Here's how to make predictions.

Clues	Prediction	New Prediction
Look for clues that hint at what's next.	Use these clues to predict what might happen next.	Adjust your predictions as you read more and find more clues.

You can try to figure out what will happen in a story even before you start reading. When you do this, you are **previewing** a story. Preview Poe's famous story by looking at the title and the illustration. What do you think might happen in this story?

Into the Story

Edgar Allan Poe is one of the best writers of horror stories. His life was short, troubled, and tragic. It's no surprise, then, that many of his tales—including this one—deal with the darkness in the human heart and mind.

THE TELL-TALE HEART

Based on the Story by

Edgar Allan Poe

Here's
HOW

NARRATOR

In lines 1–5, I learn that the narrator has been sick. He is very uneasy about something, and he may even be crazy!

Here's
HOW

MAKING PREDICTIONS

The narrator says (line 12) that he decided to kill the old man. Based on what I know about the narrator, I believe that he will. I read on and discover in line 16 that he has already killed the old man. I predict the story will describe *how* the murder was committed.

True! I had been very, very nervous, and I still am. But why do you call me insane? The disease has improved my senses, particularly my hearing. I heard everything in heaven and in earth—and even in hell. See how calmly I

5　can tell you the whole story.

I can't say how I came up with the idea, but once I'd thought of it, I could think of nothing else. I loved the old man. He had never hurt or insulted me. I didn't want his gold.

10　It was his eye! One of his eyes looked like a vulture's.[1] It was a pale blue eye with a film[2] over it. His glance made my blood run cold. So I decided to kill him and get rid of the eye forever.

Now this is the point. You think I am crazy. You should

15　have seen how carefully I made plans! I hid my feelings well. Shortly before I killed the old man, I was kinder to him than I'd ever been.

About midnight every night for a week, I turned the doorknob—oh, so gently! Then, I made an opening for my

20　head. In the opening, I put a lantern with the light covered. Next, I stuck my head through the opening. I moved very, very slowly because I didn't want to wake up the old man.

It took me an hour to get my head where I could see him. Ha! Would a madman have been as wise as this? Then, I

25　carefully opened the lantern cover so I could see the vulture eye. But every night, the eye was closed. I could not kill him until I saw his Evil Eye.

Every morning, I asked how he had slept. So you see, he would have to have been a smart man to suspect me.

30　On the eighth night, I was so still that a watch's minute

---

1. **vulture** (VUHL chuhr): large bird that eats the flesh of dead animals.
2. **film:** a thin coating.

hand moves faster than my hand. Before this moment, I had never felt how powerful and wise I was. The old man moved on the bed suddenly, as if he had been startled.[3]

35 Now, you may think that I drew back, but I knew that he could not see the door opening in the dark. Finally, I had my head in. My thumb slipped on the lantern's cover. The old man cried out, "Who's there?"

I kept still for a whole hour. During that time the old man sat up in bed, listening. Then, I heard a groan of terror. At
40 midnight on many nights, I have made that sound. I pitied the old man, but my heart chuckled.

I knew that he had been lying awake since the first noise. He had been growing more and more afraid. But there was no escape. The presence of Death made him *feel* my head in
45 the room.

I waited for a long time, very patiently. I aimed the light only on the old man's vulture eye. It was wide open.

Now, I have told you that I am not mad. Rather, my senses are too sharp. So I began to hear a low, dull, quick
50 sound, like a watch wrapped in cotton. I knew *that* sound too well. It was the beating of the old man's heart. It made me even angrier, like a drumbeat makes a soldier braver.

I held the light on the eye, but the sound of the heart grew quicker and louder. He *must* have been terrified![4] The
55 noise terrified me, too. I thought the heart would burst. And now I became afraid that a neighbor might hear the sound.

With a loud yell, I leaped into the bedroom. The old man shrieked only once. In an instant, I dragged him to the floor and pulled the heavy bed over him. Then, I smiled because
60 the deed[5] was done.

Your TURN

NARRATOR

Re-read lines 38–41 and 48–52. Then, underline one of the narrator's actions or thoughts that shows he may be mad or insane.

Your TURN

MAKING PREDICTIONS

By line 60 at the bottom of this page, the murder has been committed. What do you think the rest of the story will be about?

_____

_____

_____

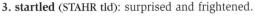

3. **startled** (STAHR tld): surprised and frightened.
4. **terrified** (TEHR uh FYD): filled with great fear.
5. **deed:** an act.

But, for a while, the heart beat on with a muffled[6] sound. Finally, it stopped. The old man was dead. I held my hand over his heart for many minutes but felt no heartbeat. He was stone dead. His eye would trouble me no more.

65 Do you still think I'm mad? Consider how I hid the body. First, I cut up the corpse. Next, I took up three boards from the bedroom floor and hid the body parts there. There were no bloodstains. I had caught all the blood in a tub. When I finished, it was four o'clock. I answered a knock at the door 70 with nothing to fear.

Three police officers entered. The officers had come because a neighbor had reported a shriek in the night.

I smiled. What did I have to fear? I said I had shrieked from a dream. Saying the old man was away, I let them 75 search the house. Then, I led them to *his* bedroom and brought chairs. I wanted them to rest *here*. I put my own chair over the place where I'd buried the old man.

My *manner*[7] had convinced the officers. We all chatted happily, but soon, I felt myself get pale. My head ached, 80 and my ears seemed to ring. I kept talking, but the feelings got worse. Soon, I realized the noise was *not* within my ears.

I am sure that I now grew *very* pale. I talked faster and louder, but the sound grew. *It sounded like a watch wrapped* 85 *in cotton*. I gasped for breath. The officers didn't hear the noise. I talked faster; the noise grew.

I stood up and paced the floor, waving my arms as I argued about nothing. But the noise steadily grew. I dragged my chair over the floorboards, but the noise arose over all 90 and grew louder and louder and *louder*!

---

6. **muffled** (MUHF uhld): covered up; made less loud.
7. **manner**: way of behaving.

Still the officers chatted and smiled. Was it possible they could not hear it? Almighty God!—no, no! They heard! They suspected! They *knew*! They were making a cruel joke of my horror! Anything was better than their knowing smiles. I

95 could bear it no more. I felt I must scream or die! And now! Again—listen! louder! louder! *louder!*

"Villains!"[8] I shrieked. "Pretend no more! I admit the deed! Tear up the floorboards! Here! Here! It is the beating of his hideous[9] heart!"

Your TURN

MAKING PREDICTIONS

Will the police officers say they heard the beating sound of the tell-tale heart? Explain your answer.

_____

_____

_____

Your TURN

MAKING PREDICTIONS

Will the narrator go to prison for his crime, or will he be sent to a mental hospital?

_____

_____

_____

---

8. **villains** (VIHL uhnz): wicked people.
9. **hideous** (HIHD ee uhs): very ugly; disgusting.

Narrator

Weighing the Narrator

The narrator of "The Tell-Tale Heart" insists he isn't mad or insane. What do you think?

Below is a scale on which you can weigh your evidence. On the right-hand side of the scale, write the evidence, or reasons, you have for thinking the narrator is insane. In the left-hand side of the scale, place the evidence you have for thinking the narrator is sane. Then, write your final judgment on the lines below the diagram. Two pieces of evidence have already been done for you.

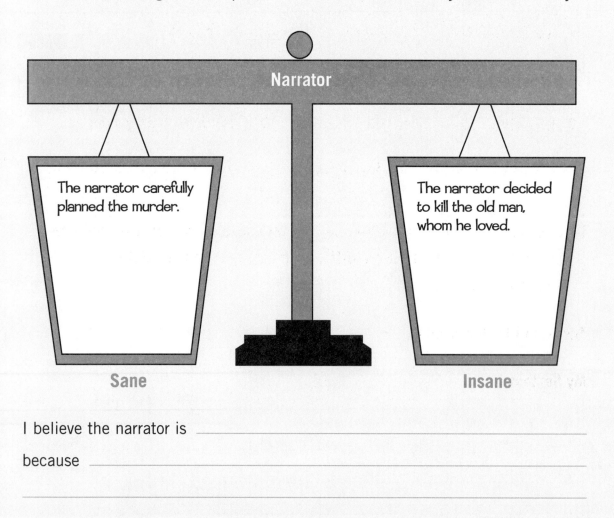

Narrator

The narrator carefully planned the murder.

The narrator decided to kill the old man, whom he loved.

Sane

Insane

I believe the narrator is _____

because _____

_____

_____

Vocabulary

Words with More than One Meaning

A. In the left-hand column below are words from "The Tell-Tale Heart." In the right-hand column are some of the definitions those words can have. Use the line number for each word to look it up in the story. Then, draw a circle around the definition that word has in the story. One has been done for you.

Word from "The Tell-Tale Heart"	Definitions
1. mad (line 48)	**a.** angry **b.** insane **c.** wild
2. ring (line 80)	**a.** to make bell sounds **b.** a finger band
3. film (line 11)	**a.** thin coating **b.** what photos are taken on
4. watch (line 84)	**a.** device for telling time **b.** to look at something

B. Choose a word from the left-hand column above. Then, write a sentence using that word. Try to use a different meaning than the word has in "The Tell-Tale Heart."

The word I have chosen is _____

My Sentence

_____

_____

_____

_____

Raymond's Run

Literary Focus: Dialect

If you live in New York, you might think that people in Texas have a different way of speaking English. They might think that you sound different, too! You are both noticing differences in dialect. **Dialect** is a way of speaking that is typical of a certain place or a certain group of people. Everyone speaks a dialect of some kind. Even if your dialect is close to standard English, it will still show regional or group differences. When you read this story, pay attention to Squeaky's dialect.

Reading Skill: Making Judgments

When you read, you are **making judgments.** This means that you are forming opinions or feelings about the people and events in the story. When you begin reading a story, you might like one character. Later, that judgment might change. Making notes on a chart like the one below will help you keep track of your judgments. A more complete version of this chart is on page 126.

Character	Early Judgment	Later Judgment
Squeaky		

Into the Story

Do you have hidden qualities and talents? Have you ever suddenly discovered a hidden talent in a friend? "Raymond's Run" is a story about discovering many things—but most importantly, finding a hidden friendship and talent.

Raymond's Run

Based on the Story by

Toni Cade Bambara

1 **I** don't have to work around the house like some girls. All I have to do is mind my brother Raymond, which is enough.

Raymond needs looking after because he's not quite right. A lot of rude people have lots to say about Raymond, 5 but they have to say it to me. I'd much rather knock you down than talk, even though I'm small and have a squeaky voice. That's how I got my name. Squeaky. If things get rough, I run. I'm the fastest thing on two feet.

There is no track meet that I don't win the first-place 10 medal. I'm the swiftest thing in the neighborhood. That goes for Gretchen, too. She says that she is going to win the first-place medal this year. What a joke. No one can beat me.

I'm walking down Broadway practicing my breathing. Raymond pretends he's driving a stagecoach.[1] That's OK 15 by me. So long as he doesn't stop my breathing exercises. I'm serious about my running.

Some people act like things come easy to them. Take Cynthia Procter. She just won the spelling bee for the millionth time. "A good thing you got 'receive,' Squeaky," 20 she says. "I would have got it wrong. I forgot to study." I could kill people like that. I stay up all night studying the words for the spelling bee. And I practice running whenever I can.

So I'm walking down Broadway breathing out and in. 25 Along come Gretchen and her two buddies. Mary Louise used to be a friend of mine. Rosie is as fat as I am skinny. She has a big mouth about Raymond. But there's not much difference between herself and Raymond. She can't afford

---

1. stagecoach: in the early days of our country, a coach, or carriage, that carried passengers and mail and was pulled by horses.

"Raymond's Run" adapted from *Gorilla, My Love* by Toni Cade Bambara. Copyright © 1971 by Toni Cade Bambara. For on-line information about other Random House, Inc. books and authors, see the Internet website at http://www.randomhouse.com. Retold by Holt, Rinehart and Winston. Reproduced by permission of **Random House, Inc.**

to throw stones. So they are coming up Broadway and the
30   street ain't that wide. I could let them pass, but that's
chicken. As they get to me, they slow down. I'm ready to
fight.

"You signing up for the May Day races?" smiles Mary
Louise. Only it's not a real smile.

35   "You're not going to win this time," says Rosie. I've beat
her up many times for insults[2] smaller than that.

"I always win because I'm the best." I say it straight at
Gretchen. Gretchen smiles, but it's not a smile. They all
look at Raymond bringing his stagecoach to a stop.

40   "What grade you in now, Raymond?"

"You got anything to say to my brother, Mary Louise
Williams? You just say it to me."

"You his mother?" Rosie says back to me.

"That's right, fatso. If anybody says another word, I'll be
45   their mother." They stand there. Gretchen stands first on
one leg and then the other. She's about to say something
but doesn't. She walks around me looking me up and down.
Then she keeps walking, and her two buddies follow her.
Me and Raymond smile at each other. He says, "Gidyap." I
50   keep on walking and doing my breathing exercises.

I take my time getting to the park on May Day. The
track meet is the last thing on the program.[3] The biggest
thing on the program is the May Pole dancing.[4] I can do
without that, thank you. Who wants to be dancing around a
55   May Pole? Getting all dirty and sweaty, acting like a fairy or
flower in a new white dress and shoes. You should be

2. **insults** (IN suhlts): rude or impolite words or actions.
3. **program** (PROH gram): the order of events.
4. **May Pole dancing:** dancing around a tall pole decorated with ribbons and
   flowers to celebrate May Day, a springtime festival that often features sports and
   games.

Here's HOW

VOCABULARY

Squeaky uses a lot of slang. For example, she uses the word *chicken* in line 31 to mean "cowardly." I like slang because it makes the person sound more real.

Your TURN

DIALECT

Re-read lines 29–30. Underline a word that is not part of standard English. (You can find this word in most dictionaries.) How would you say this entire phrase in standard English?

Here's HOW

MAKING JUDGMENTS

In lines 54–57, I learn that Squeaky really wants to be herself and not what other people want her to be. I've changed how I feel about her. I like and respect her now because she is not afraid to be herself.

Your
TURN

VOCABULARY

Read lines 72–75, and tell what the word *break* means. Underline the phrase or sentence that helps you know its meaning.

_____

_____

_____

Here's
HOW

VOCABULARY

The word *fly* in line 84 can mean "an insect" or "going really fast." Here I think it means "going really fast" because Squeaky is telling how fast she is running.

yourself. For me that means being a poor black girl who can't afford fancy shoes and a dress.

I was once a strawberry in a nursery school play. I
60 danced with my arms over my head. As expected, my mother and father came dressed up and clapped. You'd think they'd know better. I am not a strawberry. I do not dance. I run. That is what I am all about. So I always come late to the May Day program. I get my number pinned on.
65 Then, I lay in the grass till they call out the fifty-yard dash.

I put Raymond in the little swings on the other side of the fence. Then here comes Mr. Pearson, dropping things all over the place. "Well, Squeaky," he says, checking my name off the list. He hands me number seven and two pins.
70 "Hazel Elizabeth Deborah Parker." I tell him to write it down on his list.

"Going to give someone else a break this year?"

I look at him real hard. Is he joking? I should lose the race on purpose? Grown-ups got a lot of nerve sometimes.
75 I pin on number seven and stomp away.

The man on the loudspeaker announces the fifty-yard dash. Gretchen is at the starting line. I get into place. I see Raymond on the other side of the fence. He is bending down with his fingers on the ground. Just like he knew what
80 he was doing.

I spread my fingers in the dirt and crouch on my toes. I am telling myself, Squeaky you must win. You are the fastest thing in the world. At the sound of the pistol, I am off. I fly past the other runners. My arms pump up and down. I
85 glance to my left. No one. To the right, a blurred Gretchen. On the other side of the fence, Raymond is running. His arms are down to his side and the palms tucked up behind him. It's the first time I ever saw that. I almost stop to watch

my brother Raymond on his first run. But I keep going and
90 tear past the white ribbon.

I lean down to catch my breath. Here comes Gretchen.
She's gone past the finish line and is coming back. She's
taking it slow, breathing in steady. I sort of like her a little
for the first time. "In first place . . . ," the man on the
95 loudspeaker pauses. I stare at Gretchen. She stares back.
We both are wondering who won.

Raymond is yanking at the fence. Then like a dancer or
something, he starts climbing up nice and easy. I notice
how smoothly he climbs hand over hand. I remember how
100 he looked running with his arms down to his side. It came to
me that Raymond would make a very fine runner. And now
I'm smiling. I'm thinking it doesn't matter who wins the race.
I'd rather be a coach with Raymond as my champion. After
all, with a little more study I can beat Cynthia at the spelling
105 bee. And everyone says I'm the baddest thing around. I've
got a roomful of ribbons and medals and awards. But what
has Raymond got to call his own?

I'm laughing out loud by this time. Raymond jumps
down from the fence. He runs over with his arms down to
110 the side. No one before him has this running style. My
brother Raymond, a great runner. The man on the
loudspeaker is announcing, "In first place—Miss Hazel
Elizabeth Deborah Parker. In second place—Miss
Gretchen P. Lewis." I look at her and I smile. Because she's
115 good, no doubt about it. Then she smiles. We stand there
with this real smile of respect between us. We don't practice
real smiling every day. Maybe we are too busy being
flowers or fairies or strawberries instead of something
honest and worthy of respect . . . you know . . . like being
120 people.

Your TURN

MAKING JUDGMENTS

Re-read lines 100–107. How does Squeaky change? How do you feel about Squeaky now?

_____

_____

Here's HOW

DIALECT

Squeaky is talking in dialect when she says, "I'm the baddest thing around." (line 105) I remember when I first heard a similar expression. I had just arrived in the United States. Someone said my boots were "bad," and I got angry. Then, I realized that in this person's dialect, *bad* meant *good*!

Your TURN

DIALECT

There is no such word as *baddest* (line 105) in standard English. People usually say *worst* (as in *bad, worse, worst*). In this story, however, *baddest* does not mean *worst*. Re-read the "Here's How" above. In this story, what do you think *baddest* means?

_____

Making Judgments

As you read "Raymond's Run," you **made judgments** about the characters. That is, you formed opinions about the people in the story. Your judgments may have changed by the end of the story.

To review your reading, fill out the chart below. Look at the list of characters in the first column. In the second column, write what you thought of this character at the beginning of the story. Explain why you made this early judgment by pointing to details from this story. In the third column, write what you thought of this character by the end of story. Support your later judgment with details from the story. Part of the chart has been filled in for you.

Character	Early Judgment	Later Judgment
Squeaky	I liked the way Squeaky took care of her brother; I didn't like her toughness, though. She said she would rather fight than talk. I also thought Squeaky was too conceited. She said stuff like "I'm the swiftest thing."	
Gretchen		
Raymond		

Vocabulary

Words with More than One Meaning

Read each sentence below. Then, read the definitions given for the underlined word in the sentence. Draw a circle around the definition that fits the word in the sentence. One has been done for you.

1. I could let them pass, but that's <u>chicken</u>.
   a. cowardly
   b. a hen or a rooster
   c. a kind of meat

2. "Going to give someone else a <u>break</u> this year?"
   a. rest period
   b. chance
   c. place where something is torn apart

3. At the sound of the pistol, I am off. I <u>fly</u> past the other runners.
   a. go through the air without touching the ground
   b. go fast
   c. drive an airplane

4. I almost stop to watch my brother Raymond on his first run. But I keep going and <u>tear</u> past the white ribbon.
   a. run quickly
   b. pull or rip apart

Olympic Games

Reading Skill: Making Inferences

An **inference** is a "smart guess." To make an inference, you start with what you know. Then, you add what the writer tells you. Finally, you make your guess.

Suppose your friend Sally is always losing things—her homework, her house key, her lunch money. One day, Sally is reading a book on the bus. A friend sits down beside her. Sally sets the book on an empty seat and begins to chat. Later, she can't find the book. Which inference can you make about the lost book?

    A. Sally's friend stole the book.

    B. Sally left the book on the bus.

    C. Sally's book is in her backpack.

B is the only "smart guess." It is supported by the facts. Most likely, it is also supported by what you know. You might have made the inference this way.

What You Know		Facts		Inference
Sally is always losing things.	**+**	Sally set the book down on the bus seat.	**=**	Sally left her book on the bus.

Into the Article

You've probably seen the Olympic Games on TV. The Olympics are the most important contest for athletes around the world. In the following encyclopedia article, you will learn more about the history of this much-loved event.

The Ancient Games

1 Long ago in Greece, athletic games were part of funeral ceremonies for important people. Later, games were part of festivals held in honor of the gods. The most important festival was the Olympic Games. It honored Zeus,[1] the king

5 of the gods.

The first Olympics took place in 776 B.C. at a place called Olympia. The only sport was a running race. The winner was a cook from Elis. After that, the Olympic Games were held every four years.

10 As years went by, other sports were added, such as the pentathlon. This sport is made up of jumping, running, the discus[2] throw, the javelin throw, and wrestling. Boxing and the four-horse chariot race were also added. An odd sport was a chariot race in which two mules pulled the chariot.

15 Another strange sport was a contest for trumpeters.

Then the Romans took over Greece. The games lost their religious meaning. Finally, the Romans stopped the games from taking place.

The Modern Games

20 In 1857, archaeologists[3] found the ruins of Olympia's stadium. Because of this find, a teacher from France decided to revive[4] the Olympic Games.

The first modern Olympic Games were held in Athens, Greece, in 1896. The athletes took part in nine sports. Some

---

1. **Zeus** (zoos).
2. **discus:** a round, flat object for throwing.
3. **archaeologists** (AHR kee AH luh jihsts): people who study old things.
4. **revive** (rih VYV): to bring back.

From "Olympic Games" adapted from *The World Book Encyclopedia*, 2001. Copyright © 2001 by **World Book, Inc.** Retold by Holt, Rinehart and Winston. Available at www.worldbook.com. Reproduced by permission of the publisher.

Here's HOW

MAKING INFERENCES

After reading lines 1–5, I can infer that the first Olympic games were held to honor the gods, not individual athletes.

Your TURN

VOCABULARY

Re-read lines 10–15. Then, underline the sports that were part of the pentathlon (pehn TATH lon). Remember that the prefix *penta–* means "five."

Your TURN

MAKING INFERENCES

Re-read lines 20–22. Then, read the following inference:

The teacher from France did not believe that the Greek ruins were important.

Is this inference supported by what you read? Explain your answer.

_____

_____

_____

_____

25 of these were cycling, gymnastics, tennis, swimming, and weight lifting. The first modern Olympic winner was James B. Connolly of the United States. He won the hop, step, and jump (or triple jump).

Making Inferences

When you **make an inference,** you make an educated guess. Your guess is supported by the facts from the text and by what you already know.

In the chart below, facts from "Olympic Games" are listed in the left-hand column. Read each fact and then, in the middle column, write something that you know about that fact. In the right-hand column, tell your inference—that is, tell what you infer from the fact and your personal knowledge. One has been done for you.

Fact from "Olympic Games"	What I Know	My Inference
The most important festival in ancient Greece was the Olympic Games. It honored a god named Zeus.		
Later, other sports such as the pentathlon (jumping, running, discus throw, javelin throw, and wrestling) were added.	I have seen the pentathlon on TV when I was watching the Olympics.	Many sports from the ancient Olympics are still played in the Olympics today.
One sport was a race in which two mules pulled a chariot.		

Paul Revere's Ride

Literary Focus: Rhythm

Rhythm is the beat of a poem. The strong rhythm of this poem reflects its subject—a long, fast ride on horseback. At some points, this rhythm helps you to imagine other actions, too. As you read, listen for the beat of the poem's lines. Is it slower in some parts? Is it faster in others?

Reading Skill: Re-reading

The strong rhythm of this poem may tempt you to read it quickly. However, the poem was written long ago, and some of its words and sentences may be difficult to understand. Try to read the poem slowly. If you find that you have not understood some of the lines, stop and read them again. Then, jot down what you think the lines mean.

Lines I Need to Re-read	What I Think the Lines Mean
Lines 1-3	Listen to the story of Paul Revere's ride on April 18, 1775

Into the Poem

This poem is loosely based on real events. On the night of April 18, 1775, Paul Revere and two other men set out to warn American colonists of a British attack. The next day, groups of armed colonists stood up to the British soldiers. They fought at Concord and at another town called Lexington. These were the first battles of the American Revolution.

Henry Wadsworth Longfellow

PAUL REVERE'S RIDE

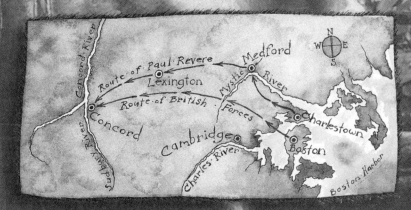

Here's
HOW

RHYTHM

When I read the first stanza out loud, I can hear the strong rhythm of the poem. It sounds like a galloping horse's hoofs. This is what it sounds like; da-da-DUM da-da-DUM.

Here's
HOW

VOCABULARY

In line 8, Revere tells his friend to hang a lantern *aloft* in the bell tower. I'm not sure what *aloft* means. I know that a *loft* is a high space. Maybe *aloft* means "high." I checked this word in a dictionary, and I was right.

1 Listen, my children, and you shall hear
Of the midnight ride of Paul Revere,
On the eighteenth of April, in Seventy-five;
Hardly a man is now alive
5 Who remembers that famous day and year.

IN OTHER WORDS Listen to the story of Paul Revere's ride. It took place at midnight, on April 18, 1775. Hardly anyone is still alive who remembers that night.

He said to his friend, "If the British march
By land or sea from the town tonight,
Hang a lantern aloft in the belfry[1] arch
Of the North Church tower as a signal light—
10 One, if by land, and two, if by sea;
And I on the opposite shore will be,
Ready to ride and spread the alarm
Through every Middlesex village and farm,
For the country folk to be up and to arm."[2]

IN OTHER WORDS Paul Revere told his friend to watch for the British. The signal that the British were coming would be a light in the bell tower of the church. One light meant the British were coming by land. Two lights meant they were coming by sea. Revere would wait with his horse on the other side of the river. If the British attacked, he would be ready to ride off and warn the local villagers and farmers to arm themselves.

---

1. **belfry** (BEHL free): tower for a bell or bells.
2. **to arm**: to get guns.

15 Then he said, "Good night!" and with muffled³ oar

Silently rowed to the Charlestown shore,

Just as the moon rose over the bay,

Where swinging wide at her moorings⁴ lay

The Somerset, British man-of-war;

20 A phantom ship, with each mast and spar⁵

Across the moon like a prison bar,

And a huge black hulk, that was magnified

By its own reflection in the tide.

IN OTHER WORDS Revere said good night to his friend. Very quietly, he rowed across the bay from Boston to Charlestown. He passed a British warship anchored in the harbor. In the moonlight, its masts looked to him like prison bars. The ship's reflection in the water made it look big and frightening.

Meanwhile, his friend, through alley and street,

25 Wanders and watches with eager ears,

Till in the silence around him he hears

The muster⁶ of men at the barrack⁷ door,

The sound of arms, and the tramp of feet,

And the measured tread of the grenadiers,⁸

30 Marching down to their boats on the shore.

IN OTHER WORDS Meanwhile, Revere's friend wandered through the streets of Boston. He looked out for the British soldiers. Finally, he heard them gather their weapons and march down to their boats on the shore.

---

3. **muffled** (MUHF uhld): sound covered up or deadened.
4. **moorings**: cables holding a ship in place so that it doesn't float away.
5. **mast and spar**: poles supporting a ship's sails.
6. **muster**: assembly; gathering.
7. **barrack** (BAR uhk): building for soldiers.
8. **grenadiers** (GREHN uh DIHRZ): foot soldiers who carry and throw grenades.

Here's HOW

RE-READ

After line 18, I lost track of what's happening. I stopped and read lines 18–23 again. They seem to say that a huge British ship is anchored in the bay and that its image is reflected in the water. Now, I'll read "In Other Words" to see if I'm right.

Your TURN

VOCABULARY

In line 19, what is a *man-of-war*? Re-read lines 18–20, and draw a circle around the word that gives you the meaning.

Your TURN

RHYTHM

When you read lines 24–27 aloud, do you begin with a slow rhythm or a fast rhythm? Why?

_____

_____

_____

VOCABULARY

I wonder what a *stealthy tread* (line 32) is. Revere's friend is climbing the wooden stairs. He's probably sneaking so the British soldiers won't hear him. Maybe *stealthy tread* means "quiet steps."

Your
TURN

RHYTHM

Re-read lines 31–39. The slower rhythm of these lines matches an action in the story. Underline the words in the poem that describe the action in lines 31–39.

Your
TURN

RE-READ

Underline one line on this page that confused you. Read the line again. Then, in your own words, write what you think the line means on the lines below.

_____

_____

_____

_____

_____

Then he climbed the tower of the Old North Church,
By the wooden stairs, with stealthy tread,
To the belfry chamber overhead,
And startled the pigeons from their perch
35 On the somber[9] rafters, that round him made
Masses and moving shapes of shade—
By the trembling ladder, steep and tall,
To the highest window in the wall,
Where he paused to listen and look down
40 A moment on the roofs of the town,
And the moonlight flowing over all.

IN OTHER WORDS   Revere's friend climbed quietly up the wooden stairs to the church tower. He woke up the pigeons roosting there, and they flew around him. Then he climbed the ladder to the highest window. There, he paused and looked down on the roofs of the town.

Beneath, in the churchyard, lay the dead,
In their night encampment[10] on the hill,
Wrapped in silence so deep and still
45 That he could hear, like a sentinel's[11] tread,
The watchful night wind, as it went
Creeping along from tent to tent,
And seeming to whisper, "All is well!"
A moment only he feels the spell
50 Of the place and the hour, and the secret dread
Of the lonely belfry and the dead;
For suddenly all his thoughts are bent
On a shadowy something far away,

---

   9. **somber:** dark and gloomy.
10. **encampment:** camping place; here, a graveyard.
11. **sentinel's** (SEHN tihn UHLZ): guard's.

Where the river widens to meet the bay—

55 A line of black that bends and floats

On the rising tide, like a bridge of boats.

IN OTHER WORDS   He looked down at the graveyard. It reminded him of a military camp, with each stone like a soldier's tent. The night wind was like a lookout, moving from tent to tent to say that all is well. It was a spooky moment. But, suddenly, in the distance, he spotted something moving on the river. It was the British warships.

Meanwhile, impatient to mount and ride,

Booted and spurred, with a heavy stride

On the opposite shore walked Paul Revere.

60 Now he patted his horse's side,

Now gazed at the landscape far and near,

Then, impetuous,[12] stamped the earth,

And turned and tightened his saddle girth;[13]

But mostly he watched with eager search

65 The belfry tower of the Old North Church,

As it rose above the graves on the hill,

Lonely and spectral[14] and somber and still.

And lo! as he looks, on the belfry's height

A glimmer, and then a gleam of light!

70 He springs to the saddle, the bridle he turns,

But lingers and gazes, till full on his sight

A second lamp in the belfry burns!

IN OTHER WORDS   Meanwhile, Paul Revere waited impatiently on the other side of the bay. He had on his

RHYTHM

Re-read lines 68–70. Is the rhythm of these lines quick or is it slow? Explain your answer.

_____

_____

VOCABULARY

The word *linger* means "to stay back." Draw a circle around what Revere is staying back or waiting to see in lines 71–72.

---

12. **impetuous** (ihm PEHCH oo uhs): impulsive; eager.
13. **girth:** strap that holds the saddle on the horse.
14. **spectral** (SPEHK truhl): ghostly.

RE-READ

Stop and re-read lines 73–80. In your own words, tell what these lines describe.

_____

_____

_____

_____

_____

_____

_____

RHYTHM

I think that I would read lines 81-86 with a firm, steady rhythm, the way a horse would slow down going up a hill. The view of the river and the ocean tides would need a smooth, flowing rhythm. I like trying out different rhythms as I read the poem.

boots and spurs. He was ready to ride. He patted his horse and he looked around. He stamped his foot. He tightened the strap of his saddle. But, mostly, he watched the bell tower of the church. It looked lonely and ghostly above the graveyard. At last, he saw a light! He jumped on his horse and turned to go. But then, he waited, and he saw the second light in the bell tower.

> A hurry of hoofs in a village street,
> A shape in the moonlight, a bulk[15] in the dark,
> 75 And beneath, from the pebbles, in passing, a spark
> Struck out by a steed[16] flying fearless and fleet:
> That was all! And yet, through the gloom and the light,
> The fate of a nation was riding that night;
> And the spark struck out by that steed, in his flight,
> 80 Kindled the land into flame with its heat.

IN OTHER WORDS The sound of hoofs hurrying through a village street. A dark shape in the moonlight. A spark made by a horseshoe striking a stone as the horse galloped by. That was all. Yet, the fate of the nation was riding with Paul Revere. The spark of freedom struck that night set the whole land on fire.

> He has left the village and mounted the steep,
> And beneath him, tranquil[17] and broad and deep,
> Is the Mystic,[18] meeting the ocean tides;
> And under the alders[19] that skirt its edge,
> 85 Now soft on the sand, now loud on the ledge,
> Is heard the tramp of his steed as he rides.

---

15. **bulk:** shape.
16. **steed:** horse.
17. **tranquil** (TRANG kwuhl): peaceful.
18. **Mystic:** Mystic River.
19. **alders:** a type of tree.

IN OTHER WORDS He left the village behind and rode up a hill. Below him was the water. He rode along the shore of the Mystic River, under the alder trees. Sometimes the hoofbeats were soft in the sand. Sometimes they were loud on rock.

It was twelve by the village clock,
When he crossed the bridge into Medford town.
He heard the crowing of the cock,
90 And the barking of the farmer's dog,
And felt the damp of the river fog,
That rises after the sun goes down.

IN OTHER WORDS At midnight, he crossed the bridge into Medford. He heard a rooster crow. He heard a farmer's dog bark. He felt the dampness of the night fog from the river.

It was one by the village clock,
When he galloped into Lexington.
95 He saw the gilded[20] weathercock[21]
Swim in the moonlight as he passed,
And the meetinghouse windows, blank and bare,
Gaze at him with a spectral glare,
As if they already stood aghast[22]
100 At the bloody work they would look upon.

IN OTHER WORDS At one o'clock, he rode into Lexington. He saw a weather vane turn. The windows of

I wasn't quite sure how Revere could know what time it was. After re-reading lines 87–90, I figured out that he looked at the clock that must have been for the whole village. Maybe there weren't many clocks and watches back then.

Your
TURN

RE-READ

Re-read lines 95–97. Circle the two things Revere sees as he rides through Lexington.

20. **gilded:** coated with gold.
21. **weathercock:** weather vane shaped like a bird.
22. **aghast** (uh GAST): struck with horror.

RE-READ

Stop and re-read lines 107–110. Who is being described in these lines?

_____

_____

_____

RHYTHM

In lines 111–118, the rhythm of these lines helps me imagine the fighting between the colonists and the British.

the meetinghouse seemed to stare at him like ghosts. It was as if they were already horrified by the bloodshed they would see.

It was two by the village clock,

When he came to the bridge in Concord town.

He heard the bleating of the flock,

And the twitter of birds among the trees,

105 And felt the breath of the morning breeze

Blowing over the meadows brown.

And one was safe and asleep in his bed

Who at the bridge would be first to fall,

Who that day would be lying dead,

110 Pierced by a British musket ball.[23]

IN OTHER WORDS At two o'clock, he came to Concord. He heard sheep bleating. He heard birds chirping in the trees. He felt the morning breeze blowing over the grass. One man, safe asleep in his bed, would be the first to die in battle that same day.

You know the rest. In the books you have read,

How the British Regulars[24] fired and fled—

How the farmers gave them ball for ball,

From behind each fence and farmyard wall,

115 Chasing the redcoats down the lane,

Then crossing the fields to emerge again

Under the trees at the turn of the road,

And only pausing to fire and load.

---

23. **musket ball:** ammunition that was fired from the muskets, or long-barreled guns.

24. **British Regulars:** British soldiers.

You know the rest. You've read about it in books. The British soldiers fired, then ran away. The farmers chased them off, shooting at them, pausing only to reload their guns.

So through the night rode Paul Revere;
120 And so through the night went his cry of alarm
To every Middlesex village and farm—
A cry of defiance and not of fear,
A voice in the darkness, a knock at the door,
And a word that shall echo forevermore!
125 For, borne[25] on the night wind of the Past,
Through all our history, to the last,
In the hour of darkness and peril and need,
The people will waken and listen to hear
The hurrying hoofbeats of that steed,
130 And the midnight message of Paul Revere.

IN OTHER WORDS So Paul Revere rode through the night. He spread the alarm all across Middlesex. It was a cry of defiance, not fear. A voice in the darkness, a knock at the door, and a word that will echo forever. For, all through our history, at times of danger, the people will wake up to the sound of that horse's hoofbeats, and the midnight message of Paul Revere.

Your
TURN

VOCABULARY

In line 122, *defiance* means "refusal to obey." Underline any words in that line that could help you figure out this meaning.

Your
TURN

VOCABULARY

If Revere hadn't warned the colonists, they would have been in great danger. Underline a word in line 127 that means "danger."

---

25. borne: carried.

Rhythm

The **rhythm** of a poem is its beat.

In each box below are two lines from the poem that have a strong rhythm or beat. Test out this rhythm by tapping it out with a pencil on a table or desk. Is the beat slow or fast? The two lines from the poem can help you imagine a certain action. What pictures do the words create in your imagination? Whom can you see? What is happening?

In each thought bubble, tell what action the rhythm helps you imagine. One thought bubble has been done for you.

1. "Meanwhile, his friend, through alley and street, / Wanders and watches with eager ears" (lines 24–25)

2. "By the wooden stairs, with stealthy tread, / To the belfry chamber overhead" (lines 32–33)

I can see Revere's friend slowly climbing up the steps. The stairs creak.

3. "A hurry of hoofs in a village street, / A shape in the moonlight, a bulk in the dark" (lines 73–74)

Vocabulary

Synonyms

A **synonym** is a word that means the same, or nearly the same, as another word. Read the sentences below. Then, choose a synonym from the word bank for each boldfaced word. Write the synonym in the blank at the end of the sentence. One has been done for you.

Word Bank
protest
sneaky
horrified
peaceful
high
wait
danger

1. The summer afternoon was lazy and **tranquil.** _____

2. No one could hear her **stealthy** steps in the hallway. _____

3. The kite soared **aloft** in the sky. _____ high _____

4. If you **linger** for long, you may miss your bus. _____

5. We were **aghast** at the damage the tornado had done. _____

6. When Meg realized she'd been cheated, she raised her voice in **defiance.**

_____

7. Hikers should avoid the **peril** of poison ivy by wearing long pants.

_____

The Cremation of Sam McGee

Literary Focus: Ballad

A **ballad** is a song or songlike poem that tells a story. The old ballads are songs that were passed on orally for many years before they were written down. The authors of most old ballads are unknown. Ballads have certain features that make them easy to memorize:

- simple language
- repeated lines
- simple rhyme schemes
- regular beat, or rhythm

All of these sounds patterns make ballads fun to sing or read aloud.

Tall Tales and Exaggeration

A **tall tale** is a story that is obviously untrue but is told as if it were completely true. The key part of all tall tales is **exaggeration**—stretching the truth as high and wide as it will go. *It was so hot, you could fry an egg on the sidewalk* is an example of exaggeration. Tellers of tall tales love to amaze and amuse with exaggerations like that one.

Into the Ballad

"The Cremation of Sam McGee" is not an old ballad. After all, we know who wrote it. However, the poem follows the old ballad form. Just like old ballads, this ballad is fun to memorize and recite or sing with a group of people. In fact, the story of Sam McGee has been recited around many campfires over the years.

The Cremation of of

Sam McGee

Robert W. Service

YOU NEED TO KNOW **Background.** Gold was discovered in the 1890s in far northwestern Canada. It was found in an area called the Klondike, in the Yukon Territory. The town of Dawson became the capital of the Yukon Territory. Thousands came to the Klondike and Dawson from all over the world. They were looking for the gold. The gold seekers were faced with long, bitterly cold winters. The snow was deep, and they had to use dogs to pull their sleds along the trails.

1 There are strange things done in the midnight sun
　By the men who moil[1] for gold;
The Arctic trails have their secret tales
　That would make your blood run cold;
5 The Northern Lights[2] have seen queer sights,
　But the queerest they ever did see
Was that night on the marge[3] of Lake Lebarge
　I cremated Sam McGee.

IN OTHER WORDS The opening refrain, which is repeated at the end of the poem, tells you that the story is set in the Yukon—the land of the midnight sun. Because the Yukon is so far north, the sun does not set in the summer. It comes down and touches the horizon and then begins to rise for the new day. At midnight, the sun still shines—the land of the midnight sun. The opening refrain also tells us that the story is about the strange cremation of Sam McGee. Cremation is the burning of a dead body. The speaker is an important character—he is the one that carries out the cremation.

---

1. **moil:** labor; work hard.
2. **Northern Lights:** bands of light that sometimes appear in the night sky of the northern hemisphere.
3. **marge:** edge.

Now Sam McGee was from Tennessee, where the cotton
 blooms and blows.
Why he left his home in the South to roam 'round the Pole,
10   God only knows.
He was always cold, but the land of gold seemed to hold
 him like a spell;
Though he'd often say in his homely[4] way that he'd
 "sooner live in hell."

On a Christmas Day we were mushing our way over the
 Dawson trail.
Talk of your cold! through the parka's fold it stabbed like a
 driven nail.
If our eyes we'd close, then the lashes froze till sometimes
15   we couldn't see;
It wasn't much fun, but the only one to whimper[5] was Sam
 McGee.

IN OTHER WORDS   Sam McGee is a gold prospector
from the southern state of Tennessee. He hates the cold
climate but stays because he hopes to strike it rich and
find gold. On Christmas Day, Sam and his partner are
sledding over the Dawson trail. The town of Dawson is the
center of the Yukon region, where miners can buy
supplies. It is so cold that the men's eyelashes freeze and
blind them. Sam is the only one to complain.

And that very night, as we lay packed tight in our robes
 beneath the snow,
And the dogs were fed, and the stars o'erhead were
 dancing heel and toe,

---

4. **homely:** simple.
5. **whimper:** to cry in a low voice.

Here's HOW

EXAGGERATION

In the line that begins
"Though he'd often say"
(line 12), McGee says he
would rather live in hell
than be cold. I think this
is an exaggeration.

Here's HOW

VOCABULARY

In the line that begins "On a
Christmas Day" (line 13), I
think I know what *mushing*
means. In the north, they use
dogs to pull sleds and to get
the dogs going, they yell
"Mush." They were being
pulled along on a sled by
dogs.

Your TURN

BALLAD

Ballads have simple rhyme
schemes that make them
easy to remember. Read
aloud lines 13–16. Notice
that the first and second
lines rhyme, as do the third
and fourth lines. Circle the
rhyming words at the end of
each line.

THE CREMATION OF SAM MCGEE   **147**

He turned to me, and "Cap," says he, "I'll cash in[6] this trip, I guess;

And if I do, I'm asking that you won't refuse my last

20   request."

Well, he seemed so low that I couldn't say no; then he says with a sort of moan:

"It's the cursèd cold, and it's got right hold till I'm chilled clean through to the bone.

Yet 'tain't being dead—it's my awful dread of the icy grave that pains;

So I want you to swear[7] that, foul or fair, you'll cremate my last remains."

IN OTHER WORDS   That night, Sam tells his partner, Cap, that he believes he will die on this trip. He begs Cap to grant Sam one last request and Cap agrees. Sam explains that he isn't afraid of dying. It's being buried in the cold ground that he dreads. He begs Cap to cremate him—to burn Sam's dead body to ashes.

A pal's last need is a thing to heed, so I swore I would not

25   fail;

And we started on at the streak of dawn; but God! he looked ghastly pale.

He crouched on the sleigh,[8] and he raved[9] all day of his home in Tennessee;

And before nightfall a corpse[10] was all that was left of Sam McGee.

---

6. **cash in:** die.
7. **swear:** to make a solemn promise.
8. **sleigh** (slay): sled that is being pulled by the dogs.
9. **raved:** talked wildly.
10. **corpse:** dead body.

There wasn't a breath in that land of death, and I hurried, horror-driven,

With a corpse half hid that I couldn't get rid, because of a
30   promise given;

It was lashed[11] to the sleigh, and it seemed to say: "You may tax[12] your brawn[13] and brains,

But you promised true, and it's up to you to cremate those last remains."

IN OTHER WORDS Cap swears to carry out Sam's last wishes. The next day, they set off at dawn. As the day goes on, Sam becomes weaker—he is pale, and he seems out of his head, talking about his Tennessee home. At the end of the day, Sam is dead. Cap can't get rid of the corpse. He ties the body to the sled where it constantly reminds him of his promise to cremate Sam.

Now a promise made is a debt unpaid, and the trail has its own stern code.

In the days to come, though my lips were dumb, in my heart how I cursed that load.

In the long, long night, by the lone firelight, while the
35   huskies, round in a ring,

Howled out their woes to the homeless snows—O God! how I loathed[14] the thing.

And every day that quiet clay seemed to heavy and heavier grow;

Your
TURN

EXAGGERATION

Re-read lines 29–32. How does the author use exaggeration here to make his story seem even more frightening?

_____

_____

Your
TURN

VOCABULARY

The word *dumb* in line 34 can mean "foolish or stupid" or "silent." Underline the meaning you think *dumb* has here.

Your
TURN

BALLAD

Ballads often repeat phrases, words, and even sounds. In lines 29–37 of this ballad, the *h* sound is repeated many times. Circle all the words on this page that begin with the *h* sound.

---

10. **corpse:** dead body.
11. **lashed:** tied.
12. **tax:** put a strain on.
13. **brawn:** muscle.
14. **loathed** (loh*th*d): hated; despised.

And on I went, though the dogs were spent[15] and the
    grub[16] was getting low;
The trail was bad, and I felt half mad, but I swore I would
    not give in;
And I'd often sing to the hateful thing, and it hearkened[17]
40   with a grin.

IN OTHER WORDS   A promise must be carried out—this is the way the men who live in the frozen north live. So Cap keeps moving along with Sam's dead body on the sled. However, at night, with the dogs howling around the fire, Cap admits that he hates the body of Sam McGee. As each day goes by, the body seems to grow heavier. Food for the dogs is running out, and the trail is rough. Still, poor Cap can't get rid of the body. He sings to the body and it seems to hear him—and grin.

Till I came to the marge of Lake Lebarge, and a derelict[18]
    there lay;
It was jammed in the ice, but I saw in a trice[19] it was
    called the "Alice May."
And I looked at it, and I thought a bit, and I looked at my
    frozen chum;[20]
Then "Here," said I, with a sudden cry, "is my
    cre-ma-tor-ium."

---

15. spent: worn-out.
16. grub: food supplies.
17. hearkened (HAHR kuhnd): listened.
18. derelict (DEHR uh lihkt): abandoned ship.
19. in a trice: quickly.
20. chum: friend.

Some planks I tore from the cabin floor, and I lit the boiler
  45   fire;
Some coal I found that was lying around, and I heaped the
        fuel higher;
The flames just soared, and the furnace roared—such a
        blaze you seldom see;
And I burrowed a hole in the glowing coal, and I stuffed in
        Sam McGee.

IN OTHER WORDS   At last Cap comes to a ruined
boat that is frozen into the ice at Lake Lebarge. He looks
at the wooden boat, he looks at the frozen body of Sam—
and he has an idea. The boat will be his crematorium—
the place where he can burn Sam's body. Cap sets fire to
wood in the boiler, adds some coal that is lying around,
and soon has a blazing fire. He makes a hole in the coals
that are alight and stuffs Sam McGee's body into the fire.

Then I made a hike, for I didn't like to hear him sizzle so;
And the heavens scowled, and the huskies[21] howled, and
  50   the wind began to blow.
It was icy cold, but the hot sweat rolled down my cheeks,
        and I don't know why;
And the greasy smoke in an inky cloak[22] went streaking
        down the sky.

I do not know how long in the snow I wrestled with
        grisly[23] fear;
But the stars came out and they danced about ere again I
        ventured near;

---

21. **huskies:** sled dogs.
22. **cloak:** covering.
23. **grisly** (GRIHZ lee): horrible.

VOCABULARY

What do you think a boiler is (line 45)? Underline the word in line 47 that tells you what a boiler is.

Here's HOW

BALLAD

Hey, I see another type of repetition here! It's not a repeated word, phrase, or sound. It's the sentence structure. In line 45, the sentence structure is not usual. Normally, I'd say that line this way: "I tore some planks from the cabin floor" (subject-verb-object). I think it sounds funny when the ballad repeats that same unusual structure in line 46.

EXAGGERATION

Sometimes writers use personification—making a thing or object do what people do—to add excitement to their exaggeration. Underline the words in line 50 where the writer has used this technique.

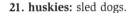

I was sick with dread, but I bravely said: "I'll just take a
55   peep inside.
I guess he's cooked, and it's time I looked"; . . . then the
    door I opened wide.

IN OTHER WORDS Cap leaves the burning fire because he doesn't like to hear the sizzling noise of the baking body of Sam McGee. The sky is dark, the dogs howl, and the wind blows cold. Cap sweats as he wrestles with his fear and dread. It is night before he can bring himself to return to the boat and open the door of the boiler.

And there sat Sam, looking cool and calm, in the heart[24] of
    the furnace roar;
And he wore a smile you could see a mile, and he said:
    "Please close that door.
It's fine in here, but I greatly fear you'll let in the cold and
    storm—
Since I left Plumtree, down in Tennessee, it's the first time
60   I've been warm."

There are strange things done in the midnight sun
    By the men who moil for gold;
The Arctic trails have their secret tales
    That would make your blood run cold;
65 _The Northern Lights have seen queer sights,_
    But the queerest they ever did see
Was that night on the marge of Lake Lebarge
    I cremated Sam McGee.

---

24. heart: center; middle.

IN OTHER WORDS Sam is sitting calmly in the middle of the blazing fire, warm at last. He tells Cap to close the boiler door because he doesn't want any cold air coming in. Then, we hear once again the opening stanza. It reminds us of the setting and of the strangeness of the story of the cremation of Sam McGee.

BALLAD

Now that you've read the ballad, you can go back and memorize the **refrain,** the stanza that's repeated at the opening and closing of the poem. Say the first line of the refrain aloud several times. Then, try saying it aloud without looking at the page. Then, do the same for the second line. Now, put both lines together. Eventually, you can add the next two lines, and so on. If you're really ambitious, you can ask several classmates to take a stanza to memorize. Then, you all can take turns reciting each stanza of the ballad aloud.

Summarizing the Ballad

In each of the boxes below is an event in the ballad of "The Cremation of Sam McGee." However, the events are not in order. Carefully read each event. Then number them in the order in which they happened in the ballad. The first event has been numbered for you.

_____ Sam dies.

_____ Cap cremates Sam's body in an abandoned ship.

___1___ Sam makes Cap promise to cremate him if he dies.

_____ Cap has to carry Sam's body on his sled for several days.

_____ Sam is alive and happy to be warm.

Vocabulary and Comprehension

In each of the exercises below, one item has been done for you.

A. Complete each sentence with one of these words:

whimper (page 147) **derelict** (page 150) **boiler** (page 151)

heart (page 152)

1. Cap pushed the corpse of Sam McGee right into the

_____ of the fire.

2. Cap tears up some planks and lights a fire in a _____ boiler _____.

3. Sam McGee is the only one to _____ because of
the cold.

4. Cap uses a _____ as his crematorium for burning the
body of Sam McGee.

B. Write **T** or **F** next to each statement to tell if it is **T**rue or **F**alse.

_____ **1.** The narrator promises to cremate Sam McGee if he dies.

_____ **2.** Sam McGee loves cold weather.

_____ **3.** The narrator never keeps his promise.

___T___ **4.** The narrator puts Sam on an abandoned ship and sets fire to it.

C. Answer each question below.

1. Why does Sam want to be cremated?

_____

_____

2. What happens to Sam McGee when he is cremated?

When Sam McGee is cremated, he sits up and smiles, happy to be warm at last.

_____

from Beowulf

Literary Focus: Epic

An **epic** is a long narrative poem (a *narrative poem* is a poem that tells a story). Ancient epics like *Beowulf* usually feature a superhuman hero. Today's comic book heroes, like Batman and Spiderman, give you a good idea of how powerful the epic hero is. Everything else in an epic seems larger than life, too. Other feature of the epic include

- a dangerous journey or mission
- supernatural or magical elements
- an elevated, or lofty, tone. The language of the poem is not everyday language. For example, when Beowulf, the hero of this epic, tells about the time he hunted sea monsters, he says, "death was my errand and the fate / They had earned." In everyday speech, this might translate into, "I set out to kill those sea monsters, and they deserved it, too."

As you read the selection, look for more examples of larger-than-life characters, situations, and language.

Into the Epic

Like many of the oldest epics, *Beowulf* was first an oral story. A person sang or spoke it to audiences, and it was not written down. When it was finally written down—over a thousand years ago—it was written in Old English. Old English was the language of the Anglo-Saxons who dominated the British Isles long ago. Old English is very different from the English used today, and *Beowulf* has been translated into Modern English many times.

FROM Beowulf

TRANSLATED BY

Burton Raffel

Here's HOW

EPIC

The words I underlined (in lines 6 and 7) seem to mean "at night." I guess that's what they mean when they say epics have elevated language!

YOU NEED TO KNOW Beowulf is the name of the main character of the poem. He is a warrior from the land of the Geats (in Scandinavia). Grendel is the name of a huge monster in the poem. He is killing and eating the followers of Hrothgar, a Danish king. In the section that follows, Beowulf talks to King Hrothgar. Beowulf tries to persuade the king to choose him to fight Grendel because he is the best warrior.

"Hail, Hrothgar!
Higlac is my cousin[1] and my king; the days
Of my youth have been filled with glory. Now Grendel's
Name has echoed in our land: Sailors
5 Have brought us stories of Herot, the best
Of all mead-halls,[2] deserted and useless when the moon
Hangs in skies the sun had lit,
Light and life fleeing together.

IN OTHER WORDS Beowulf says hello to Hrothgar. He introduces himself, saying that King Higlac is one of his relatives. Beowulf also says that when he was young he did many great deeds. Beowulf knows that the monster Grendel is taking over the king's land. People can't go out at night because they are afraid of Grendel. As soon as the sun goes down, people run home.

My people have said, the wisest, most knowing
10 And best of them, that my duty was to go to the Danes'

---

1. **cousin:** any relative. Higlac is Beowulf's uncle and his king.
2. **mead-halls:** Mead is a drink made from honey, water, yeast, and malt. The hall was a central gathering place where warriors could feast, listen to the bard's stories, and sleep in safety.

From *Beowulf*, translated by Burton Raffel. Translation copyright © 1963 and renewed © 1991 by Burton Raffel. Reproduced by permission of **Dutton Signet, a division of Penguin Group (USA) Inc.**

Great King. They have seen my strength for themselves,
Have watched me rise from the darkness of war,
Dripping with my enemies' blood. I drove
Five great giants into chains, chased
15 All of that race from the earth. I swam
In the blackness of night, hunting monsters
Out of the ocean, and killing them one
By one; death was my errand and the fate
They had earned.

IN OTHER WORDS Beowulf says that many wise people told him to speak to Hrothgar. These people have seen Beowulf in action, and they know how strong he is. They have seen him fight in war and capture five giants. Beowulf has also hunted ocean monsters and killed them. He says that all these enemies deserved to die.

20   Now Grendel and I are called
Together, and I've come. Grant me, then,
Lord and protector of this noble place,
A single request! I have come so far,
Oh shelterer of warriors and your people's loved friend,
25 That this one favor you should not refuse me—
That I, alone and with the help of my men,
May purge[3] all evil from the hall.

IN OTHER WORDS Now Beowulf is ready to fight a new enemy, Grendel. Beowulf compliments Hrothgar by saying the king takes care of his warriors and is loved by his people. Then, Beowulf asks Hrothgar for a favor. He wants the chance to fight Grendel and make the land safe.

---

3. purge: to get rid of, remove.

Here's HOW

EPIC

If Beowulf has all the qualities that his people most admire, they must have really admired fighters. This Beowulf seems a little too powerful to be true. He would need magical powers to swim out in the ocean and hunt monsters (lines 15–17). In fact, then whole situation is supernatural. I mean, there are no sea monsters, right?

Your TURN

EPIC

1. In lines 20–27, underline an example of elevated language. Then, translate those words into everyday words:

_____

_____

2. In these same lines, Beowulf asks permission to do something. What is he asking to do?

_____

_____

3. Beowulf's request will most likely lead to
a. an elevated tone
b. a dangerous mission
c. a great feast

FROM **BEOWULF**   **159**

The Granger Collection, New York.

Your TURN

EPIC

In lines 28–36, Beowulf explains why he feels he should fight Grendel with his bare hands. Underline his reason(s). Then, based on these lines, put check marks next to the qualities listed below that apply to Beowulf.

bravery
faith
cleverness
pride
strength
generosity

I have heard,

Too, that the monster's scorn of men

30 Is so great that he needs no weapons and fears none.

Nor will I. My lord Higlac

Might think less of me if I let my sword

Go where my feet were afraid to, if I hid

Behind some broad linden shield:[4] My hands

35 Alone shall fight for me, struggle for life

Against the monster. God must decide

Who will be given to death's cold grip.

IN OTHER WORDS Beowulf has heard that Grendel doesn't fear men. The monster doesn't even use weapons because he thinks he's so much stronger than men. Beowulf says that he won't use weapons, either. His king, Higlac, won't be impressed if Beowulf uses his sword or hides behind a big shield to protect himself. So, Beowulf says he'll use only his hands to fight against Grendel. God will decide which of the two will die.

---

4. linden shield: shield made from wood of the linden tree.

Qualities of the Epic Hero

Have you ever heard of a poster child? A poster child is any person that represents a group or a cause. It's not hard to imagine Beowulf as a poster child for the Anglo-Saxons. After all, an epic hero mirrors the qualities most valued by the people who created that hero.

Imagine that you live in an Anglo-Saxon world threatened by swamp creatures and fire-breathing dragons. Beowulf can't fight these monsters alone anymore—he needs the help of a few good men and women. In the space below, make a poster promoting the Anglo-Saxons' cause. Beowulf, of course, should be at the center of the poster. He's looking for people that share his qualities. What are those qualities? Represent the qualities with symbols, phrases from the epic, sketches of epic scenes, or all three.

Langston Hughes: A Biography

Reading Skill: Writing a Summary

A **summary** is a shortened version of a text. A summary gives the main idea of the text. It also includes the important details that support the main idea. Here is a checklist of what goes into a good summary.

A Good Summary Includes:

☐ the **title** of the text

☐ the **main idea** of the text

☐ the **important details** that support that main idea

Into the Article

Langston Hughes was born in Joplin, Missouri, in 1902. He began writing poetry in his early teens. As a young man, he traveled around the world and held many jobs. In 1967, Hughes died in Harlem in New York City. Read this biography of Langston Hughes to learn more about this important African American poet.

Langston Hughes:
A Biography

1 **A**ccording to a popular story, the poet Langston Hughes first became famous when he was twenty-three years old. He was working as a busboy[1] in a restaurant. Vachel Lindsay,[2] a famous poet, came to eat at the restaurant.

5 Hughes left three of his poems by Lindsay's plate. Lindsay was so impressed that he read them that night at a public reading. Lindsay said that he had discovered a true poet, a young black man working as a busboy. For the next few days, newspapers praised the "busboy poet."

10 That is a good story but it's misleading.[3] Hughes was not an overnight success. He had written poetry since grade school and was first published in his high school literary magazine. Hughes had already seen many of his poems published in journals and magazines. A book of his poetry,

15 *The Weary Blues,* was soon to be published by a famous New York publisher.

Here's
HOW

VOCABULARY

I wasn't sure of the meaning of the word *biography*. I looked it up in a dictionary. It means "the history of a person's life." I noticed that there were a lot of words on the same page, all beginning with *bio*. I looked *bio* up and it means "life."

Here's
HOW

SUMMARY

The first two lines of this biography tell me that Langston Hughes was a famous poet. I'll have to read on to find out more about how he became famous.

Your
TURN

SUMMARY

Re-read lines 10–16. Then, in lines 10–11, underline an important detail that tells you more about how Hughes became a famous poet.

---

1. **busboy:** a waiter's helper.
2. **Vachel Lindsay:** (VAY chuhl).
3. **misleading** (mihs LEE dihng): causing a wrong conclusion.

Your
TURN

VOCABULARY

Re-read line 30. Then, find
another word in that line
that helps you understand
the meaning of *illuminate*.
Draw a circle around that
word.

Your
TURN

SUMMARY

The main idea of this short
biography is that Langston
Hughes is one of our most
famous African American
poets. Re-read lines 22–27
and underline one detail
that supports this main
idea.

After meeting Lindsay, Hughes went on to become a
highly successful writer. He worked in Harlem, in New York
City. This was during the Harlem Renaissance[4]—a time when
20 many talented poets, musicians, and artists lived and worked
there.

Hughes believed that an artist's work should help all
people see the beauty within themselves. Hughes also wrote
about the experiences of African Americans. He imitated the
25 rhythms of jazz and the blues in some of his most famous
poems. He helped set up black theater companies and wrote
plays for them to perform.

Langston Hughes is one of the most famous and original[5]
of all African American poets. He said his work was an
30 attempt to "explain and illuminate the Negro condition[6] in
America." Hughes succeeded in that and more: His work
celebrates the condition of all people everywhere.

---

4. **renaissance** (REHN uh SAHNS): rebirth.
5. **original** (uh RIHJ uh nuhl): creative; having new ideas.
6. **condition** (kuhn DIH shuhn): position in life.

Writing a Summary

A **summary** is a shortened version of a text. A summary gives the main idea of the text. It also includes the important details that support the main idea.

A Good Summary Includes:

☐ the **title** of the text

☐ the **main idea** of the text

☐ the **important details** that support that main idea

Below is the beginning of a summary of "Langston Hughes: A Biography." Go back to page 163 and re-read the words you underlined for the Your Turn on that page. Then, add another sentence to the summary on the lines below.

"Langston Hughes: A Biography": Summary

Hughes became famous when he was twenty-three years old. Another poet named Vachel Lindsay read a few of Hughes's poems at a public reading.

Ribbons

Literary Focus: The Speaker

The **speaker** is the voice that tells you a story or talks to you in a poem. (In a story, this voice is more often called the **narrator.**) It is important to remember that the speaker is not the writer. In "Ribbons," for example, the speaker is a young girl named Stacy, but a man named Laurence Yep wrote this story. So, obviously here the speaker is not the writer.

Reading Skill: Asking Questions

Good readers **ask questions** as they read.

When you have a question about what you are reading, stop! See if there are any clues in the story that can help you answer your question. Sometimes you may have questions about historical details that appear in a story. For such questions, you may need to look for answers in a source outside the story. Other times you won't find a simple answer to your question. In this case, you can bring your question to your classmates and start a lively discussion.

Into the Story

The grandmother and granddaughter in this story grew up in very different cultures. Is your childhood different from or similar to the childhoods of your grandparents or parents? How? Think about things such as homes, games, chores, schools, clothes, music, and fads.

Ribbons

BASED ON THE STORY BY

Laurence Yep

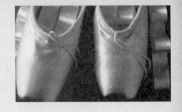

1 **I** was practicing my ballet in the living room. A car stopped outside. Ian, my little brother, rushed to the window. "Paw-paw's here!" he shouted. *Paw-paw* is Chinese for grandmother.

5 Mom had been trying to get her mother to come from Hong Kong to San Francisco for years. Grandmother had finally agreed, but only because the British were going to return the city to the Chinese Communists in 1997. Grandmother's airfare and legal expenses had been very high.

10 As a result, there wasn't any more money for my daily ballet lessons.

The rear car door opened. A pair of carved black canes poked out. "Wait, Paw-paw," Dad said.

Grandmother, however, was already using her canes to get

15 to her feet. "I'm not helpless," she told Dad.

Ian was relieved. "She speaks English," he said.

"She worked for a British family for years," Mom explained.

Grandmother was a small woman in a padded silk jacket

20 and black pants. Her hair was pulled back into a bun behind her head. On her small feet she wore a pair of quilted cotton slippers shaped like boots.

"What's wrong with her feet?" I whispered to Mom.

"They've always been that way. And don't mention it,"

25 she said. "She's sensitive about them."

Mom had told us her mother's story often enough. When Mom's father died, Grandmother had strapped my mother to her back and walked across China to Hong Kong to escape the Communists who had taken over the country. I had

---

"Ribbons" by Laurence Yep adapted from *American Girl* magazine, January/February 1992. Copyright © 1992 by **Laurence Yep.** An expanded version of "Ribbons" was published by G.P. Putnam in 1996. Retold by Holt, Rinehart and Winston. Reproduced by permission of the author.

30 always thought her trek was heroic. But it seemed even braver when I realized how wobbly she was on her feet.

The weeks after my Grandmother arrived, I felt lost. Grandmother was staying in my room, and Mom started laying down all sorts of new rules. First, we couldn't run 35 around or make noise because Grandmother had to rest. Then, we couldn't watch our favorite TV shows because Grandmother couldn't understand them.

Worst of all, Ian got all of her attention—and her candy and anything else she could give him. When I complained to 40 Mom about how Grandmother was spoiling Ian, she only sighed. "He's a boy, Stacy. Back in China, boys are everything."

I guessed that Grandmother favored Ian because he looked more Chinese. I looked more Caucasian, like my dad.

45 Even so, I kept telling myself, Grandmother is a hero. She'll like me just as much as she likes Ian once she gets to know me. And, I thought, the best way to know a person is to know what she loves. For me, that was the ballet.

Ever since Grandmother had arrived, I'd been practicing 50 my ballet privately in the room I now shared with Ian. Now I got out the special box that held my satin toeshoes. I had been so proud when I was ready to use them. I was the youngest girl on *pointe* in my ballet school. I slipped one of the shoes onto my foot. But when I tried to tie the ribbons 55 around my ankles, the ribbons came off in my hands. I decided to go ask Grandmother to help me.

"Paw-paw," I said, "can you help me?"

Grandmother gave a start when she turned around and saw the ribbons dangling from my hand. Then she looked

Your TURN

THE SPEAKER

By now, you've learned a lot about the speaker. List two new things you learn about Stacy on this page.

1. _____

2. _____

Here's HOW

ASKING QUESTIONS

You're probably curious about the statement Stacy's mother makes in lines 41–42. What question would you ask about this statement?

_____

_____

Where can you can find out if this statement is true?

_____

What else would you like to know about this statement? Write another question below.

_____

_____

_____

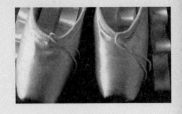

60 down at my bare feet. They had calluses from three years of daily lessons. She looked at the ribbons with hate and disgust.

"Give those to me," she said. "They'll ruin your feet." She tried to grab them away from me.

65 Angry and confused, I stepped back. I showed her the shoe. "No, they're for dancing!"

"Lies!" she said. She came toward me.

"It's the truth!" I backed up so fast that I bumped into Mom as she came running from the kitchen. By this point, I

70 was in tears. "She's taken everything else. Now she wants my toeshoe ribbons."

Grandmother looked at Mom. "How could you do that to your own daughter? Take them away! Burn them!"

Mom sighed. "Yes, Mother."

75 I couldn't believe it. "Aren't you going to stand up for me?" I shouted at Mom.

"Can't you see how worked up Paw-paw is?" Mom whispered. "She won't listen to reason. Give her some time." She took the ribbons and the shoe from my hands.

80 For the rest of the day, Grandmother just turned away every time Mom or I tried to raise the subject of the ribbons.

That evening, I finally said to Mom, "She's so weird. What's so bad about satin ribbons?"

"They remind her of something awful that happened to

85 her. But she made me promise never to talk about it."

The next evening, I happened to go into the bathroom. The door wasn't locked, so I thought no one was in there. But Grandmother was sitting on the edge of the bathtub. She had her feet soaking in a pan of water.

90 "Don't you know how to knock?" She said and dropped a towel over her feet.

Still, I had caught a glimpse of her bare feet. They were like taffy that someone had stretched out and twisted. Each foot bent downward in a way that feet were not meant to.

95 Her toes stuck out at odd angles, more like lumps than toes. I didn't think she had all ten of them, either.

"What happened to your feet?" I whispered in shock.

Looking ashamed, Grandmother flapped a hand in the air in front of me. "None of your business. Now get out."

100 That night Mom came in and sat on my bed. "Your grandmother's very upset, Stacy," she said.

"I didn't mean to look," I said. "It was horrible."

Mom said, "She was so ashamed of them that she didn't like even me to see them."

105 "What happened to them?" I wondered.

"There was a time back in China when people thought women's feet had to be shaped a certain way to look beautiful," Mom said. "When a girl was five, her mother would gradually bend her toes under the sole of her foot."

110 "Ugh," I said. "Her own mother did that to her?"

"Her mother and father thought it would make their little girl attractive so she could marry a rich man."

I shook my head. "There's nothing lovely about those feet."

115 "I know. But they were usually bound up in silk ribbons. Because they were a symbol of the old days, Paw-paw undid the ribbons as soon as we were free in Hong Kong—even though they kept back the pain."

I was even more puzzled now. "How did the ribbons do 120 that?"

"The ribbons kept the blood from circulating freely and bringing more feeling to her feet. Once the ribbons were gone, her feet ached. They probably still do. She doesn't want you to feel the same pain she felt."

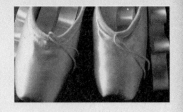

Your
TURN

THE SPEAKER

In line 131, why does Stacy
stop reading?

_____

_____

_____

_____

_____

Your
TURN

THE SPEAKER

Why do you think the author
chose a young girl to tell
this story? Explain your
answer below.

_____

_____

_____

_____

_____

125   I guess Grandmother loved me in her own way. She came into the bedroom with Ian later that evening.

    Ian asked me to read him "The Little Mermaid." So, I opened my old collection of fairy tales.

    When Grandmother and Ian sat down on my bed, I began
130 to read. However, when I got to the part where the Little Mermaid could walk on land, I stopped.

    Ian was impatient. "Come on, read," he ordered.

    "After that," I went on, "each step hurt her as if she were walking on a knife." I couldn't help looking up at
135 Grandmother.

    "I would rather have kept swimming," Ian said.

    "But maybe she wanted to see new places and people by going on the land," Grandmother said softly. "If she had kept her tail, the land people might have made fun of her."

140   When she glanced at her own feet, I thought she might be talking about herself. So, I took my chance. "My satin ribbons aren't like your old silk ones. I use them to tie my toeshoes on when I dance." Setting the book down, I got out my other shoe. "Look."

145   I began to dance before Grandmother could stop me. "See? I can move fine."

    She took my hand and patted it. It was the first time she had shown me any sign of affection. "When I saw those ribbons, I didn't want you feeling pain like I do."

150   "Let me have my ribbons and my shoes," I said in a low voice. "Let me dance."

    "Yes, yes," she whispered.

    I realized she was crying. Then I began crying, too.

    "So much to learn," she said. "So much to learn."

Asking Questions

As you read "Ribbons," you asked many questions. Some of your questions had to do with the characters and what was happening in the story. Maybe you found the answers to these questions in the story itself. Other questions had to do with historical and factual details in the story. For answers to these questions, you needed to look at sources outside the story.

Charting Historical Details

Chart your reading below. Re-read the lines from the story listed in the first column. In the second column, write one of your questions about the historical details you found in these lines. In the third column, write where you can find an answer. Finally, look at your source, and write what you found out. The first row has been filled in for you.

Lines in Story	One Question	Where To Look for an Answer	What I Found Out
Lines 6–8	Where is Hong Kong?	dictionary; atlas	Hong Kong is on the South China Sea. It's in the southeast part of China.
Lines 41–42			
Lines 106–124			

Getting to the *Pointe*

Reading Skill: Unity and Text Structure

> Hey, Kate,
>
> You won't believe what happened to me today. I was practicing doing an ollie on my skateboard. You know, crouch down, spring up, hands in the air. It's kind of like jumping off a diving board. I wish they would fix the diving board at the city pool. First of all, swimming is boring if you can't dive. And "B," diving and skateboarding are the best sports in the world . . .

Are you having trouble following this letter? That's because it lacks *unity* and a clear *text structure.*

A text has **unity** when all of its details support a main topic. The letter above has no particular topic.

Texts are easier to understand when they follow a pattern, or **text structure.** Here are some examples:

Chronological order: In this pattern, events are described in the order that they happen. A biography is usually written in this order.

Order of importance: A writer supporting her opinion with reasons might present her reasons from least to most important, or from most to least important.

Logical order: In this pattern, ideas are arranged in categories. When a review discusses a movie by looking at different parts—main characters, soundtracks, and costumes, for example—it has a logical order.

Getting to the *Pointe*

based on the article by Sheri Henderson

When you think of extreme sports, what's on your list? Snowboarding? Rock climbing? Ballet?. . .What? Not ballet? Think again. A ballet dancer must have the balance of a snowboarder and the strength of a rock climber. A ballet
5 dancer also has to be as flexible as a gymnast. Ballet dancers are artists, but they also have to be first-rate athletes.

The *Pointe*—A Platform the Size of a Silver Dollar

Ballet dancers perform on the *pointe* of their toeshoes. The
10 tip of a toeshoe is about the size of a silver dollar. It's very hard and seems as if it has a block of wood in it. What's really in it? Most toeshoes are made from paper. The paper is soaked in glue and then shaped. Finally, it is covered in satin. At first, the shoes are stiff, but they break down easily
15 when used. These shoes do not give the foot much padding or protection. But they do allow the dancer to "feel" the floor.

The Floor—It Should Protect the Dancer

Most of the stages where dancers perform were designed for
20 opera, not dance. Their wood floors are often laid directly on concrete or steel beams. As a result, they lack the spring that would protect a dancer's legs and feet. To see for yourself, try doing jumping jacks on concrete. Then, try again on dirt or lawn. Your legs, ankles, and feet will feel
25 the difference in these surfaces.

Here's HOW

VOCABULARY

My mother danced on toe shoes. She called it "dancing on *pointe*." *Pointe* is just the French spelling for *point*, as in the point of your foot. We pronounce it "*point*" in this country, but in France they say "pwant."

Here's HOW

UNITY AND TEXT STRUCTURE

It looks like each subhead tells what the paragraph below it is about. In the paragraph to the left, all the details are about the surfaces athletes and dancers perform on. That gives the paragraph unity.

I wonder what the overall text structure is? It's not chronological. I can tell because the writer is not telling a story that unfolds over a period of time.

Ballet—A Risky Art

A dancer must follow a long, demanding training program. Correct form and technique are very important to avoiding injury. A good ballet teacher corrects the tiniest errors in
30 foot placement. Young dancers may long for toeshoes, but good ballet teachers know that this step must not be rushed. Experts suggest that *pointe* work should not begin before ages ten to twelve. Before then, the feet are still growing.

Dance—A Conversation Between Dancer and Audience

35 Ballet dancers work hard, but they must make their dancing look easy. Dance is an art form, so it is not judged by the same standards as athletic contests are. The longest leap doesn't win a medal. The length of the leap is less important than the way the dancer leaps. The dancer's leap
40 must be powerful and graceful at the same time. Dancers are able to enchant an audience with the power of their movement. A leap becomes a sentence in a conversation between the dancer and the audience. When audience members are so involved in the conversation that they
45 forget to notice that the leap itself is spectacular, the dancer has been successful.

Why Do It?

Why snowboard? Why rock climb? There are so many risks! But athletes would probably answer that they do it for the
50 freedom and joy they feel in challenging their limits. There is also a thrill that comes with enchanting an audience. For ballet dancers, the joy of performing their art is as necessary as breathing.

Text Structure

Taking a Closer Look

In "Getting to the *Pointe*," the writer uses logical order to show that ballet dancing is an extreme sport. She looks at several categories, or topics of information, related to ballet dancing. In the cluster diagram below, identify the main idea the author makes about each topic. Then, note a detail the author uses to support each main idea. (Some parts of the organizer have been filled in for you.) Finally, agree or disagree with the overall main idea. Explain your answer.

Balance

Main Idea:

Details:

Working in difficult conditions

Main Idea: Most stage floors are hard on dancers' bones and joints.

Details:

Ballet is an extreme sport.

Demanding training

Main Idea:

Details:

Being both an artist and an athlete

Main Idea:

Details: Audience members caught up in dance don't realize the strength required to perform it.

I agree / disagree (circle one) that ballet dancing is an extreme sport because

_____

_____

The Treasure of Lemon Brown

Literary Focus: The Writer's Background

Sometimes you can get more out of a story if you know where a writer comes from and what he or she values. Before you read "The Treasure of Lemon Brown," be sure to read Into the Story (below). It may help make the characters in the story come alive for you.

Reading Skill: Retelling

To be sure you understand a story, stop from time to time to **retell** in your own words what has happened so far. Try pausing after each page and telling a partner what has happened. Take notes in a chart like this one. A more complete version of the chart is on page 185.

On the first page . . .	Greg and his father . . .
On the second page . . .	Greg meets Lemon Brown and . . .

Into the Story

Although Walter Dean Myers was born in West Virginia, he was raised by foster parents in New York City. Myers says that his foster father gave him a precious gift: his love. His foster mother taught him the value of education, even though she had little education herself. She also taught him that a story could be a gift.

Myers feels that young people learn a lot of negative values from the media. He believes in sharing the positive values he learned from his loving foster parents with his young readers.

The Treasure of Lemon Brown

Based on the Story by
Walter Dean Myers

Here's
HOW

**AUTHOR'S
BACKGROUND**

In lines 6 and 7, Greg's
father says he had to leave
school when he was thirteen.
He wants Greg to work
harder in school. Greg
seems mad about that. I
know that Walter Dean
Myers's foster mother didn't
get much education, but she
still taught Myers to value
his education. Maybe Greg
will understand his father's
point of view later on.

Here's
HOW

RETELLING

I'll make sure I understand
what has happened so far
by retelling the events. First,
Greg feels angry that he
is failing math and that his
father won't let him play
basketball. Next, he walks
down the street and into
an old apartment building.
While he thinks about his
father, Greg is surprised by
someone who says he has a
razor.

The dark sky was filled with angry, swirling clouds. Greg Ridley was sitting on the front steps of his apartment house. His angry mood matched the clouds as he remembered his father's voice reading out the letter. It was from the

5   principal, saying that Greg would probably fail math.

"I had to leave school when I was thirteen," his father had said. "I wish I'd had half the chances that you have."

Greg had sat at the kitchen table, listening to his father. He knew that now his father would not allow him to play

10   basketball. The Scorpions, the Community Center team, wanted Greg on their team, although he was only fourteen. It was the chance of a lifetime. That chance ended with the letter from the principal.

Greg knew he should go upstairs and study his math

15   book. Instead, he walked down the street to the abandoned[1] tenement.[2] He noticed that the door was slightly open. He pushed it gently and let himself in.

In the front room, Greg could see an old table, what looked like a pile of rags in the corner, and a broken-down

20   couch. He went to the window and stood looking out at the rain. He thought about the Scorpions, and then his father. Greg's father was a postal worker. He was proud of his job. He often told Greg how hard he had worked to pass the test. Greg had heard the story too many times.

25   What was that sound? Greg held himself still and listened intently.[3] It was someone breathing!

Slowly he turned around.

"Don't try nothing. I got a razor here!"

---

1. **abandoned** (uh BAN duhnd): deserted; left empty and unused.
2. **tenement** (TEHN uh muhnt): an old, run-down apartment house.
3. **intently:** with concentration.

"The Treasure of Lemon Brown" by Walter Dean Myers adapted from *Boy's Life Magazine,* March 1983. Copyright © 1983 by Walter Dean Myers. Retold by Holt, Rinehart and Winston. Reproduced by permission of **Miriam Altshuler Literary Agency, on behalf of Walter Dean Myers.**

Greg held his breath, peering[4] at the figure that stood
30 before him.

"Who are you?" said Greg.

"I'm Lemon Brown," came the answer. "Who are you?"

"Greg Ridley."

The figure shuffled[5] forward, and Greg saw an old man
35 with a black, wrinkled face, crinkly white hair, and whiskers.
He wore several dirty coats and baggy pants. From the
knees on down, his legs were covered in rags tied with
string. There was no sign of a razor.

Greg relaxed. He had seen the man before, picking
40 through the trash.

"You ain't one of them bad boys looking for my
treasure, is you?" Lemon Brown asked.

"I'm not looking for your treasure," Greg answered,
smiling. "If you have one."

45 "Every man got a treasure," Lemon Brown said. "You
know who I am?"

"Your name is orange or lemon or something like that."

"Sweet Lemon Brown," the old man said, pulling back
his shoulders as he did so. "They used to say I sung the
50 blues[6] so sweet that if I sang at a funeral, the dead would
start rocking with the beat.[7] Used to travel all over. You ain't
never heard of Sweet Lemon Brown?"

"Afraid not," Greg said.

Lemon Brown looked toward the window. "What's that
55 noise?"

Greg peered out and saw three men. One was carrying
a length[8] of pipe.

Here's HOW

WRITER'S BACKGROUND

The man Greg describes in lines 34-38 must be a homeless man. There are lots of homeless people in my city. I read that Walter Dean Myers was raised in New York City; there's probably lots of homeless people there too. Greg recognizes this man, which is why he isn't scared.

Your TURN

RETELLING

In your own words, retell to a partner what has happened on this page or write it on another sheet of paper.

---

4. **peering:** looking closely.
5. **shuffled** (SHUHF uhld): dragged feet while walking.
6. **blues:** a slow, sad form of jazz music.
7. **beat:** rhythm.
8. **length** (lehngkth): a piece of something that is long, such as a board or a pipe.

THE TREASURE OF LEMON BROWN

Your TURN

RETELLING

On this page, Lemon Brown and Greg face three men who demand Lemon Brown's "treasure." What does Greg do?

_____

_____

What does Lemon Brown do?

_____

_____

Here's HOW

VOCABULARY

I'm not sure what the word _eerie_ in line 80 means. At first I thought it might mean "funny" or "strange." But then Greg tries to make Lemon Brown seem _eerier_ by howling and scaring the men. If something is _eerie,_ then it must be both strange _and_ frightening.

"They's bad men," Lemon Brown whispered, leading Greg into the hallway and up the darkened stairs.

60   There was a banging downstairs and a light as the three men entered. "Hey! Ragman!" one called out. "We come to get your treasure."

"We won't hurt you," said another voice. "Unless we have to."

65   "You sure he's here?"

"I don't know," came the answer. "All I want is his treasure. He might be like the shopping-bag lady with that money in her bags."

"You think he's upstairs?"

70   "HEY, OLD MAN, ARE YOU UP THERE?"

Silence.

"Watch my back, I'm going up."

Greg held his breath. He thought about the pipe, wondering what he would do when the man reached them.

75   Then Lemon Brown stood up at the top of the stairs, both arms raised high above his head.

"There he is!" a voice cried from below.

"Throw down your treasure, old man, so I won't have to bash your head in!"

80   Lemon Brown didn't move. He was an eerie sight, a bundle of rags standing at the top of the stairs. His shadow loomed[9] over him. Maybe, the thought came to Greg, I can make this scene even eerier.

Greg wet his lips, put his hands to his mouth, and
85 howled.

"What's that?"

As Greg howled, Lemon Brown hurled[10] himself down the stairs. There was a crashing noise, yelling, and running

---

9. loomed: appeared in a frightening form.
10. hurled: threw suddenly and violently.

footsteps. The front door opened and slammed shut. Then
90 there was only silence.

"Mr. Brown?" Greg called. "You OK?"

"Yeah. I got their flashlight," came the answer.

"They wanted your treasure." Greg ran down the stairs.

"You want to see it?" From his layers of ragged
95 clothing, Lemon Brown produced a piece of folded plastic
and carefully unfolded it. Inside were yellowed newspaper
clippings[11] and a battered harmonica.[12]

"There be my treasure," he said.

Greg began to read the clippings about Lemon Brown,
100 a blues singer and harmonica player who played in shows
more than fifty years ago. Greg looked at the harmonica. It
was dented badly on one side.

"I used to travel around and make money to feed my
wife and Jesse—that's my boy's name. He grew up to be a
105 man and went off to fight in the war. I gave him these things
that told him who I was and what he come from. If you know
your pappy did something, you know you can do something,
too. Then Jesse got killed. Broke my heart, it truly did."

Greg didn't know what to say, so he just nodded.

110 "They sent back what he had with him over there," said
Lemon Brown. "This old mouth fiddle and these clippings.
When I give it to him, he treated it just like a treasure. Ain't
that something?"

"Yeah, I guess. . . . I mean, you're right."

115 "You OK for a youngster." Lemon Brown carefully
wrapped the clippings and the harmonica in the plastic.
"Better than those bad men what come here looking for my
treasure."

---

11. **clippings:** pieces cut from a newspaper.
12. **harmonica** (hahr MAHN ih kuh): small musical instrument that is held in the hand and played by the mouth.

Your TURN

VOCABULARY

In line 97, Lemon Brown's harmonica is described as *battered*. Circle the words in line 102 that help you figure out the meaning of *battered*.

Here's HOW

VOCABULARY

In line 111, Lemon Brown talks about a mouth fiddle. I think that this is just another name for a harmonica.

Your TURN

RETELLING

In your own words, retell the last thing that happens on this page.

_____

_____

_____

_____

_____

_____

_____

THE TREASURE OF LEMON BROWN   **183**

"Is your treasure really worth fighting for against men
120 like that? And a pipe?"

"What else a man got excepting what he can pass on to his child?" Lemon Brown said. "You get home now."

"You sure you'll be OK?" Greg asked.

"I'll be heading west in the morning," Lemon Brown
125 said.

"You take care of that treasure."

"That I'll do," Lemon said.

The rain had stopped. Greg climbed his front steps and pushed the button over the bell marked "Ridley." He thought
130 of the lecture[13] that he knew his father would give him, and smiled.

---

13. lecture (LEHK chuhr): a scolding; talking to.

Retelling Chart

Use the chart below to retell the key events in the story. Then, use your notes in the chart to retell the story out loud to a partner. (When you are retelling the story out loud, you won't say "On the first page . . . on the second page. . . ." Instead, you will say, "First . . . Then . . . Suddenly . . . " and so on.) You can use the margin notes from pages 180 to 184 to help you complete the chart. Part of the chart has been completed for you.

On the first page	Greg and his father have just had a talk about Greg's failing math. Greg feels angry that he is failing math and that his father won't let him play basketball. Next, he walks down the street and into an old apartment building. While he thinks about his father, Greg is surprised by someone who says he has a razor.
On the second page	Greg meets Lemon Brown and . . .
On the third page	Greg and Lemon Brown face three men who want Lemon Brown's "treasure." First, Greg . . . Then, Lemon Brown . . .
On the fourth page	The men run away and . . .
On the fifth page	Greg asks Lemon Brown . . .

Leash-Free Dog Run Documents

Reading Skill: Reading Documents

Our world is full of written information. Web sites, newspapers, manuals, reports, labels—you see written documents almost everywhere you turn. Knowing what kind of document you are reading can help you understand the information it gives.

In this selection, you will read two different types of documents. **Public documents** give information about public organizations and not-for-profit groups. These documents can be about community issues, special events, or any number of other subjects. **Workplace documents** tell you information you need to know to do your job.

Into the Documents

Most people would say that dog owners should walk their pets on a leash. But, what do you think about having special places where dogs can run free? Read what these documents have to say about this issue!

Based on the Documents by
Sheri Henderson

Leash-Free Dog Run Documents

Location: http://www.southpaws.com/home

SouthPaws

1   Welcome to the SouthPaws Web-site. SouthPaws is a not-for-profit group. We want to create and maintain a leash-free space on the south

5   side of our city for its 165,000 canine (that's dog) citizens. Please consider joining our 3,300+ members. Your membership fees[1] are tax-deductible[2] and will help give our dogs their own space! If you are interested in

10 volunteering, please check out <u>Volunteer Want Ads</u>. Finally, you might want to consider SouthPaws T-shirts, sweatshirts, caps, or leashes as a gift or for yourself. All proceeds support SouthPaws.

What's New?

    Congratulations to the hundreds of volunteers who

15 gathered signatures on the SouthPaws petition. The people who live in our city have voted to set up a park or a beach where our dogs can run unleashed. This space will be jointly paid for by the city and SouthPaws donations.[3]

20 SouthPaws volunteers will supervise[4] the space during daylight hours and will ticket dog owners who do not observe cleanup and safety rules. We will have one trial[5] year after the space officially opens to prove that the idea works. Now we need your help more than ever.

---

1. **fees:** money paid to be a member.
2. **tax-deductible** (TAKS dih DUHK tuh buhl): able to be subtracted from one's taxable income.
3. **donations:** gifts (usually in the form of money) to not-for-profit organizations.
4. **supervise:** watch over; manage.
5. **trial:** practice.

SouthPaws

We are working with the city Parks and Recreation Department to choose a location. These are the most likely locations.

Cameo Park

Pro
- is centrally located
- has convenient access roads[6]
- has street parking

Con
- will have high maintenance costs
- is smallest, at 1.2 acres[7]
- is now a popular family park
- may lead nearby residents[8] to object to noise

Rocky Point Beach

Pro
- is little used
- consists of 5 nonresidential[9] acres
- has enough parking
- will have low start-up and maintenance costs

Con
- is inconveniently located
- has small sand beach and a larger area of smooth but potentially[10] slippery rocks

Main Beach

Pro
- is centrally located
- consists of 7.3 nonresidential acres
- has sand beach

Con
- is heavily used all year
- may cause conflicts with businesses
- has limited, costly parking
- will require 24-hour security and maintenance staffing
- will have high maintenance costs

<u>Pick a Site</u> Click here to cast your vote in our survey.

Your TURN

READING DOCUMENTS

Which site do you think is the best choice for the "unleashed" space? Underline the pros and cons that helped you decide. Then, explain your answer below.

---

6. **access** (AK sehs) **roads:** small roads that run along and lead to a major road.
7. **acres** (AY kuhrz): units of land, each equal to 43,560 square feet.
8. **residents** (REHZ uh duhnts): those who live in a place.
9. **nonresidential** (NAHN reh zuh DEHN shuhl): a place where people do not live and that is used mostly for business.
10. **potentially** (puh TEHN shuh lee): possibly, but not yet actually.

SouthPaws

South Paws • 1111 South P Street • South City, CA • 90123

1   December 12, 2004
Ms. T. Wagger
Director of Parks and Recreation
2222 Central Avenue
5   South City, CA 90123

Dear Ms. Wagger:

SouthPaws members would like you to consider their concerns when choosing the site of the dog run. Here they are, in order of importance:

10   **1. Space.** Healthy dogs need a large enough space in which to run. The park needs to be large enough for many dogs to run around in it without bumping into one another.

2. Conflicts. A site that is already popular for sports, family activities, or tourism will likely be a problem.

15   **3. Site.** Our research shows that dog beaches are preferable[1] to dog parks. Dogs are hard on park grass. They turn the grass to mud in rainy weather. Also, sand or shells can be brushed off a dog, but a muddy dog requires a bath. Dog beaches are also easier to supervise and clean.

20   Thank you for working with us to find a solution that is in the best interests of the most people. We are looking forward to meeting with you next week.

Sincerely,

A. K. Nine

25   A. K. Nine
Chairperson
SouthPaws Site Committee

---

1. preferable (PREH fuh ruh buhl): better liked.

Reading Documents

Business Letter

Imagine that you are T. Wagger, Director of Parks and Recreation. You want to respond to the SouthPaws member who wrote you a letter. Complete the business letter below.

2222 Central Avenue
South City, CA 90123

December 14, 2004

A. K. Nine
Chairperson, Site Committee
SouthPaws
1111 South P Street
South City, CA 90123

Dear A. K. Nine:

Thank you for your letter. It is important for us to work together to choose a good leash-free site. Our office is in favor of the site at _____. Here are three of our reasons:

1. Space: _____

_____

2. Conflicts: _____

_____

3. Type of Area: _____

_____

Thank you for working with us on this issue. I look forward to seeing you at the meeting next week.

Sincerely,

T. Wagger
Director, Parks and Recreation

Computers

Reading Skill: Following Technical Directions

When you want to do something new, you usually follow directions. To cook pasta, you might read the directions on the box. To do yoga stretches, you might follow the directions on a video.

To do something a little more complicated, such as building a model, you would follow **technical directions.** Technical directions are often included when a process has many steps or parts. These directions lay out the steps you must follow to put the object together or to make it work. If a step is skipped or done at the wrong time, the item may not work. It might even break!

Use this checklist when you are following technical directions:

Before you begin, read the directions all the way through.	✓
Check off the steps one by one as you complete them.	✓
Compare your work with the diagrams and drawings for each step.	✓

Into the Article

Have you ever opened a huge computer box only to find a tangle of wires, plugs, and strange parts? The following article explains the parts of a computer. It also shows how to put your computer together. Read the article slowly and carefully. When it's time to unpack the box, you'll be ready to go!

COMPUTERS

Based on the Article from

Holt Science
and Technology

1 Did you use a computer to wake up this morning? You might think of a computer as something you use to send e-mail or surf the Net, but computers are around you all the time. Computers are in automobiles, VCRs,[1] and telephones.

5 Even an alarm clock is a computer! An alarm clock lets you program the time you want to wake up, and it will wake you up at that time.

What Is a Computer?

A **computer** is an electronic machine that performs tasks by

10 processing and storing information. A computer performs a task when it is given a command and has the instructions necessary to carry out that command. Computers do not operate by themselves, or "think."

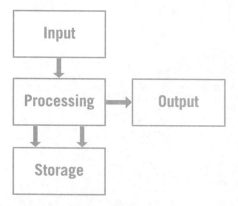

Figure 1
The Functions of a Computer

Basic Functions The basic functions a computer performs

15 are shown in **Figure 1.** The information you give to a computer is called *input.* Setting your alarm clock is a type of input. To perform a task, a computer *processes* the input, changing it to a desirable form. Processing could mean adding a list of numbers, making a drawing, or even moving

20 a piece of equipment. Input doesn't have to be processed immediately; it can be stored until it is needed.

---

1. **VCRs:** <u>v</u>ideo <u>c</u>assette <u>r</u>ecorders.

Computers store information in their *memory*. For example, your alarm clock stores the time you want to wake up. It can then process this stored information by going off at the programmed time. *Output* is the final result of the task performed by the computer. What's the output of an alarm clock? The sound that wakes you up!

Computer Hardware

For each function of a computer, there is a matching part of the computer where each function occurs. **Hardware** refers to the parts, or equipment, that make up a computer. As you read about each piece of hardware, refer to **Figure 2**.

Input Devices Instructions given to a computer are called input. An *input device* is the piece of hardware that feeds information to the computer. You can enter information into

Your
TURN

**TECHNICAL
DIRECTIONS**

Re-read lines 33–37. Suppose you want to feed some information into a computer. Underline five tools you might use to do this.

Figure 2 Computer Hardware

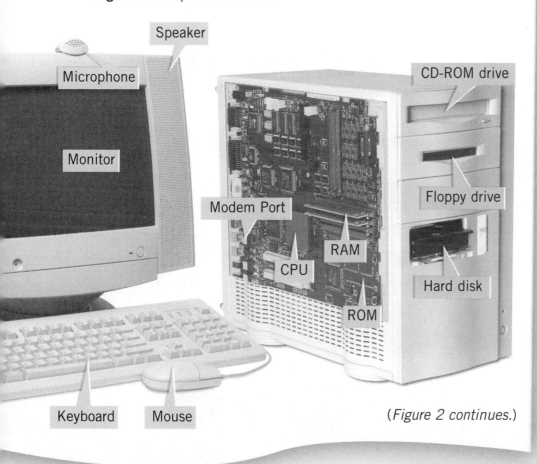

Speaker

Microphone

CD-ROM drive

Monitor

Modem Port

Floppy drive

RAM

CPU

Hard disk

ROM

Keyboard

Mouse

(*Figure 2 continues.*)

Your
TURN

TECHNICAL DIRECTIONS

In which part of a computer is its work performed?

_____

_____

Your
TURN

VOCABULARY

The word *permanent* (line 49) means "lasting a long time." Underline the clue in lines 50–54 that helps you know this meaning.

Your
TURN

VOCABULARY

Now circle a word in line 53 that means the opposite of *permanent.*

Your
TURN

TECHNICAL DIRECTIONS

Re-read lines 47–57. What is the difference between ROM and RAM?

_____

_____

a computer using a keyboard, a mouse, a scanner, a digitizing pad and pen—even your own voice!

Central Processing Unit A computer performs tasks within an area called the *central processing unit,* or CPU. In a
40 personal computer, the CPU is a microprocessor. Input goes through the CPU for immediate processing or for storage in memory. The CPU is where the computer does calculations, solves problems, and performs the instructions given to it.

Memory Information can be stored in the computer's
45 memory until it is needed. Hard disks inside a computer and floppy disks or CD-ROMs inserted into a computer have memory to store information. Two other types of memory are *ROM* (read-only memory) and *RAM* (random-access memory). ROM is permanent. It handles functions such as
50 computer start-up, maintenance, and hardware management. ROM normally cannot be added to or changed. It cannot be lost when the computer is turned off. On the other hand, RAM is temporary. It stores information only while that information is being used. RAM is

Figure 2 Computer Hardware (*continued*)

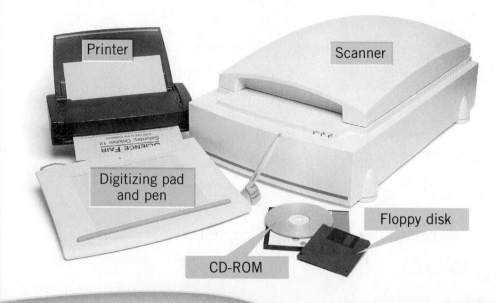

55 sometimes called working memory. Large amounts of RAM allow more information to be input, which makes for a more powerful computer.

Output Devices Once a computer performs a task, it shows the results on an *output device.* Monitors, printers, and
60 speaker systems are all examples of output devices.

Modems One piece of computer hardware that serves as an input device as well as an output device is a *modem.* Modems allow computers to communicate. One computer can input information into another computer over a
65 telephone line, as long as each computer has its own modem. As a result, modems permit computers to "talk" with other computers.

How to Set Up a Computer

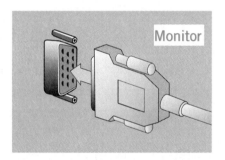

Monitor

Step 1
70 **Connect the monitor to the computer.**
The monitor has two cords: One cord, the **monitor interface cable,** lets the computer communicate with the monitor. It connects to the video port at the back of the computer. The connector on this cord is a plug with pins in it; the pins line
75 up with holes in the video port on the computer. This cable probably has screws to secure the connection. The other cord is the **monitor's power cord,** which plugs into the wall

TECHNICAL DIRECTIONS

Re-read lines 61–67. What does a modem do?

_____

_____

_____

_____

_____

_____

TECHNICAL DIRECTIONS

Circle the names of the two cords that connect to the monitor. Then underline what each cord does (lines 70–78).

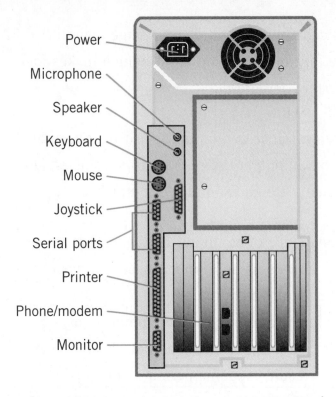

Power
Microphone
Speaker
Keyboard
Mouse
Joystick
Serial ports
Printer
Phone/modem
Monitor

outlet or **surge protector.** A surge protector is a plug-in device that protects electronic equipment from high-voltage
80 electrical surges (see Step 5).

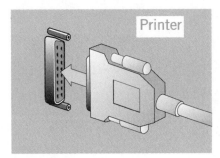

Printer

Step 2

Connect the printer to the computer.

The cable connectors for the printer have pins like those on the monitor cable and are usually secured with screws.
85 Connect one end to the back of your printer and then connect the other end to the back of your computer where you see a **printer icon.**

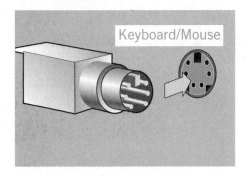

Keyboard/Mouse

Step 3

Connect the keyboard and mouse.

90 The connectors at the ends of the cords for the mouse and keyboard are round. If you look inside them, you'll see small metal pins. These pins must be lined up correctly with the holes in the ports for the parts to fit together. Do not force the connectors together. If they are not fitting properly,
95 take another look to see whether you have them lined up correctly. Plug each connector into its port on the back of your computer. The port should be labeled.

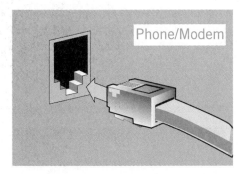

Phone/Modem

Step 4

Connect the phone line and phone to the modem.

100 Most computers come with internal modems. All you need to do is connect the wall phone jack to the phone jack on the modem. The phone jack on the modem is visible on the back of your computer. Then, plug your telephone into the other jack on the modem.

Your
TURN

TECHNICAL DIRECTIONS

Re-read lines 94–97. If you have trouble connecting the mouse to its port, what should you do?

_____

_____

_____

_____

Here's
HOW

VOCABULARY

I wonder what they mean by internal modem in line 100? The word *internal* means inside. So, an internal modem must be inside the computer.

Your TURN

TECHNICAL DIRECTIONS

Step 5 is actually a series of smaller steps. Restate each step in Step 5 below.

1. _____

_____

_____

2. _____

_____

_____

3. _____

_____

_____

4. _____

_____

_____

5. _____

_____

_____

6. _____

_____

_____

7. Turn on your computer.

Power cord

105 **Step 5**

Connect the power cords.

The power cord is a three-prong cord you attach to your computer. Attach the power cord to the computer first. Then, plug it into a surge protector. Do the same with the
110 monitor's power cord. Plug the surge protector into a wall outlet. Turn on the monitor first, then the computer, and you're ready to go!

Following Technical Directions

Ok, so you brought home the latest electronic equipment. Now what do you do? Find the directions on how to set it up! Any time you want to set up complex equipment, make sure you read the directions slowly and carefully. One way to practice reading technical directions is to write directions for how to set up something you know well. Pick some task that you know how to do, such as setting the alarm on a digital clock. You may not need all the boxes below.

Sequence Chart: Writing Technical Directions

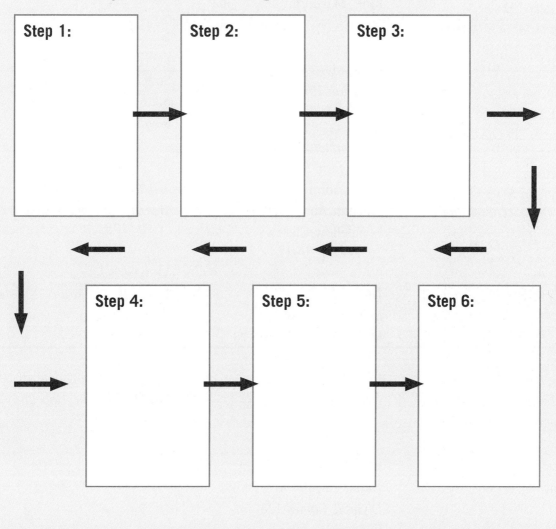

AUTHOR AND TITLE INDEX